Since you h...
a special h...

Happy birthday from
Jim + Kris 1987

# The Book of
# OUR HOUSE

# The Book of OUR HOUSE

—

WRITTEN AND COMPILED BY

—

David Ballantine & Sylvia Weinberg

The Overlook Press
Woodstock, New York

First published in 1986 by
The Overlook Press
Lewis Hollow Road
Woodstock, New York 12498

Library of Congress Cataloging in Publication Data
Ballantine, David.
The book of our house.

1. Dwellings—Maintenance and repair—Amateurs'
manuals. I. Weinberg, Sylvia. II. Title.
TH4817.3.B35  1987     643'.7      86-18231
ISBN 0-87951-267-9

Printed in the United States of America

BOOK DESIGN BY JAYE ZIMET

*Our thanks to Sylvia's sister Gail Baillergeau*
*and to our friend Marga Enoch*
*for their warm encouragement of this project.*

# Contents

# Introduction

This book was written to fill a personal need. It began one day when we wanted to paint the outside of Sylvia's house. We didn't know what kind of paint the house already had, and we were fearful that if we used the wrong kind, it would craze or blister. Why hadn't someone, we thought, put together a book where details like this could be recorded? It would certainly help our lives run more smoothly. This missing piece of information inspired *The Book of Our House*. We set about to create a record book for vital data about our homes—facts we'd probably once known but then lost or forgot because we had no organized system for keeping track of them.

In putting together this book we have created a tool that has simplified and enhanced our daily living. It has been designed so that you may customize it to your house's needs and upkeep. In effect, you are creating an operator's manual for your home.

Having a house is an evolving experience. Remembering it, at every stage along the way, can help you remember your life. Keep the record faithfully. The more you are a good friend to this book the more it will, in turn, be a good friend to you.

While we cannot hope to make you an expert on all matters of construction and maintenance, our book can suggest relevant questions that real experts will not hesitate to answer. Once you have completed this book you will probably know enough about houses in general to be an intelligent consumer and you will have created both a tool and a keepsake for all future inhabitants.

A number of "self-help" books are rather grim. We have tried to avoid the insistently accusing tone so often found in such books. In a few places our terminology and the level of detail may seem a bit overwhelming to someone new to home ownership. Hopefully these spots are rare.

And one request: Please don't let this book become a chore. There is no need to complete it immediately and no set sequence to be followed. You have lived without this book until now and have survived. Have fun getting to know your house.

We did.

# How to Use This Book

Filling out *The Book of Our House* is not meant to be a test you can't pass. In older homes some information will not be available to you until detailed examinations have been made of obscure situations—usually during the process of renovation or repair. If this is your first home, you will doubtless be confronted with a mass of unfamiliar data. It is always best to be patient with your lack of expertise because little by little the needed information usually falls into place.

This book can be neither all-inclusive nor always relevant to anyone's particular home, so we have left room for additions and we encourage deletions that will customize it to your needs. If you're reasonably certain that you are never going to use an entry, feel free to retitle it with a self-adhering label.

Before you draw charts, floor plans, and maps we suggest making a rough sketch on scrap paper for a start. Then take measurements and enter them in appropriate places on the rough sketch. After this, you can make accurate final scale drawings.

Since this book is going to be an ongoing tool, notations that may have to be changed in the future are best entered in pencil.

You are obviously not going to be able to store, within these covers, the entire volume of information your house may generate. Hence, various envelopes are suggested throughout the book. These are not to be taken literally but are instead symbols for files that you might wish to establish—you will very likely think of others.

For quicker access to your most frequently used sections, index tabs can be added. To fill out certain sections, you could meet with other people who have the book and exchange information. A friendly way to welcome new members to the community could be to present them with copies of your resource pages.

Since you will not have the book of your house with you at all times, a small notebook can help you capture useful pieces of information for later transcription.

Should you sell your house, you might want to keep the book for sentimental reasons, as a part of your history. This does not preclude allowing a new owner to transcribe your precious and hard-won essential information into his or her own copy.

# The Book of
# OUR HOUSE

# This Book of Our House

*Here is the working
story of the house
that you are building,
buying, living in, or
even dreaming of.*

*If you wish
you might fill
these spaces
with photographs.*

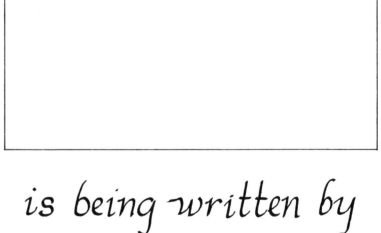

*is being written by*

_____

_____

and room for

more authors

and all those

and maybe thumb prints
if infants are involved

good people who helped
to make this possible

# Our House

address: _____

_____

_____

telephone: _____

fire number: _____

election district: _____ where we vote: _____

_____ _____

_____ _____

local school district: _____ elementary school: _____

_____ junior high school: _____

_____ high school: _____

# A House is Born

architect: _____

_____

builder: _____

sub-contractors: _____ roofing: _____

    plumbing: _____ masonry: _____

    electrical: _____ other: _____

_____

where deeds are filed: _____

place: _____

book: _____

page: _____

where house is listed on local tax rolls: _____

_____

location of deed: _____

location of original blueprint: _____

location of original plat of survey: _____

# And We Take Possession

real estate agent: _____

price of house: _____

purchased from: _____

financing the house: _____

amount of down payment: _____

details of mortgage:... mortgage # _____

    amount: _____ length: _____ interest: _____

    who holds mortgage? _____

    second mortgage?... details: _____

_____

the closing: ... date: _____

    name of our lawyer: _____

    previous owner: _____

    title guarantee insurance: _____

_____

home owners insurance: _____

agent: _____ company: _____ policy # _____

# Locations

drainfield: _____

septic tank: _____

well: _____

dry well: _____

any underground wiring? _____ if so, see wiring diagram, p.____

any underground pipes? _____ if so, see plumbing diagram, p.____

any outdoor pipes? _____ if so, see plumbing diagram, p.____

hot water heater: _____

water meter: _____

water shut-offs: _____

basement drains (if any): _____

electric meter: _____

fuse box (es): _____

circuit breakers: _____

entry to storage areas: _____

_____

in ground sprinkler heads (if any): _____

# WHOM
# TO
# CALL

# Safety Emergencies

ambulance: _____

doctor: _____

fire: _____ see p. ____ (fire # and directions to house) _____

police: state: _____

         local: _____ sheriff: _____

coast guard: _____

forest ranger: _____

game protector: _____

poison control center: _____

nearest public mental hospital _____

nearest de-toxification ward: _____

         rehabilitation center: _____

suicide emergency hot line: _____

child abuse/maltreatment reporting: _____

other local emergency hot lines: _____

_____

weather emergencies: _____

# And Those of a Personal Or Psychic Nature

mental health center: _____

v.d. counseling: _____

rape counseling: _____

battered women's services: _____

drug abuse counseling: _____

alcohol abuse program: _____

alcoholics anonymous: _____

planned parenthood: _____

_____

minister: _____

rabbi: _____

priest: _____

_____

_____

_____

# Staying Alive and Well

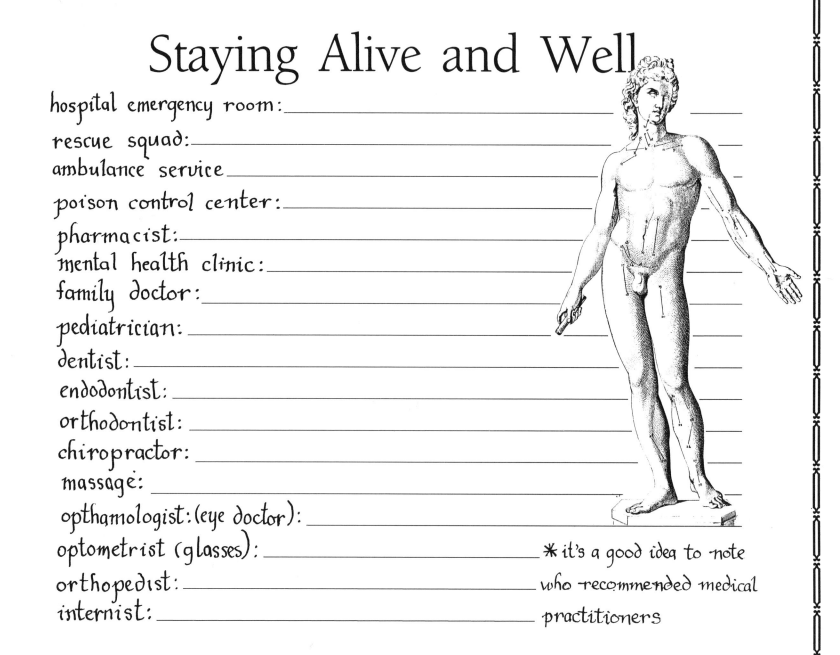

hospital emergency room: _____

rescue squad: _____

ambulance service _____

poison control center: _____

pharmacist: _____

mental health clinic: _____

family doctor: _____

pediatrician: _____

dentist: _____

endodontist: _____

orthodontist: _____

chiropractor: _____

massage: _____

opthamologist: (eye doctor): _____

optometrist (glasses): _____

orthopedist: _____

internist: _____

* it's a good idea to note who recommended medical practitioners

24

# Additional Medical Resources

gynecologist: _____

endocrinologist: _____

cardiologist: _____

urologist: _____

acupuncturist: _____

nutritionist: _____

dietician: _____

holistic practitioner: _____

homeopath: _____

hypnotist: _____

veteran's administration hospital: _____

other: _____

You sometimes hear of excellent practioners. _____

Why not store that information against _____

your own or some friend's future need.... _____

_____

_____

# Reliable Professionals

to repair or maintain the house: _____

_____

plumber: _____

electrician: _____

roofer : _____

carpenter-for repairs: _____

building contractor: _____

chimney sweep : _____

painter : _____

cabinet maker: _____

a good house cleaner : _____

_____

_____

to supply the house: _____

fire wood supplier: _____

other fuel: _____

home grocery delivery: _____

# House and Grounds

to repair or maintain the grounds:

_____
_____
_____
_____

gardener: _____

snow shoveler: _____

snow plower: _____

tree surgeon: _____

lawn mowing person: _____

garbage pick-up: _____

septic tank pumper (honey wagon): _____

driveway repair: _____

swimming pool maintenance: _____

backhoe operator: _____

_____
_____

# Specific Appliance Repair People

refrigerator: _____

freezer: _____

stove : _____

dishwasher: _____

washing machine: _____

dryer: _____

sump pump: _____

garbage disposal: _____

television: _____

audio equipment: _____

_____

_____

_____

_____

_____

# And Personal Services

barber: _____

beautician: _____

dressmaker: _____

shoe repair: _____

auto mechanic: _____

bike shop: _____

photo shop: _____

travel agent: _____

veterinarian: _____

dog walkers: _____

locksmith: _____

blacksmith: _____

ferrier: _____

baby sitters: _____

_____

_____

(this page should be written lightly in pencil, so entries can be easily changed)

# A
# DESCRIPTION
# OF
# OUR HOUSE

# Basic Specifications

details of the foundation: (i.e. slab, crawl space, full cellar, piles, stilts)

_____

| | dimensions | distance between centers | type of wood |
|---|---|---|---|
| framing details: | | | |
| wall studs: | | | |
| floor joists - 1ˢᵗ floor: | | | |
| 2ⁿᵈ floor: | | | |
| ceiling joists: | | | |
| roof rafters: | | | |

| | type | amount | date installed |
|---|---|---|---|
| insulation details: | | | |
| in outer walls: | | | |
| below floor: | | | |
| ceiling: | | | |
| other: | | | |

_____

*... strips of aluminum foil laid alongside buried plastic pipelines make it

# of This House

plumbing details: _____

    type of pipe: _____

    water supply: _____

    wastewater disposal: _____

    notes: _____

_____

electrical details: _____

    service capacity _____

    wiring method: _____

    BX, Romex, other: _____

_____

_____

_____

interior walls - details: (plaster, paneling, plaster boards etc.) _____

_____

_____

possible for a metal locator to register them . . . _____

# Making the Floor Plan

By way of example and suggestion, the following pages contain various diagrams of David's house. They are drawn to a scale of one inch to four feet. Tiny houses might use larger scales, and larger houses smaller ones. The basic floor plan can be used repeatedly, as a plumbing and then a wiring diagram. Additional copies can be retained to record various furniture arrangements and materials used for floor and wall coverings. If there are removable storm windows and doors or screens for a particular room, these may be numbered and keyed in to the plan.

A floor plan is a simple map. Most joining walls meet at right angles, and opposite walls are usually parallel. David took a steel tape and went along, adding up the window widths and the distances between, until he settled on the length of a room. Then he measured the full run with a long tape, checking this figure against the first sum until both were closely matched. Sylvia had some trouble making a floor plan for her house because she neglected to allow for the fact that external walls have thickness, and thus interior and exterior house dimensions are never the same. She was also plagued by the fact that the walls of her bedroom go off at unusual angles. David suggested that holding a protractor against one wall and a straightedge to the center of it and parallel to the wall adjacent would reveal an angle that could be transferred to her plan.

When David's house was in its earliest planning stage, he made a scale model of it out of shirt cardboards that he now wishes he had saved, if only for sentimental reasons. Were he ever to build another house, he would make a one-inch-to-one-foot scale model; whatever time and energy it took would be paid back many times in avoided mistakes. By putting some scale-model suitcases into a scale-model attic, for example, it may become apparent that the access has been designed for a world inhabited by adults under three feet in height. Or again, you may find that if the kitchen had been only two feet longer, there would have been room for a neatly vented hood above the cooking range, and that several wall switches and electrical outlets would have been much more accessible.

If your house has any eccentricities, they should be noted. Most houses do. The glass exit door from one downstairs bedroom in David's house still needs some steps down to the terrace. And speaking of terraces, Sylvia's was built before the house got lived in, and its location turned out not to be suited to the household's needs. As a result it has always been empty.

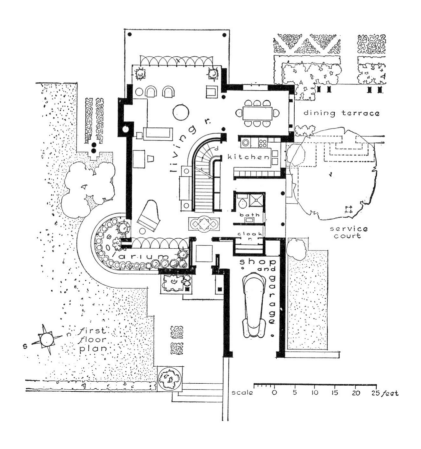

# The Floor Plan of David's House

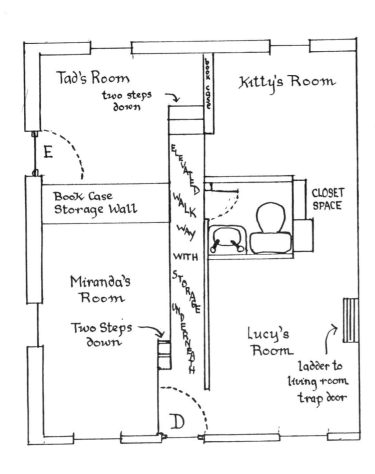

Tad's Room

two steps down

Book Case

Kitty's Room

E

ELEVATED WALK WAY WITH STORAGE UNDERNEATH

Book Case Storage Wall

CLOSET SPACE

Miranda's Room

Two Steps down

Lucy's Room

ladder to living room trap door

D

CRAWL SPACE

under kitchen floor

C

← the downstairs children's rooms are underneath the living room.

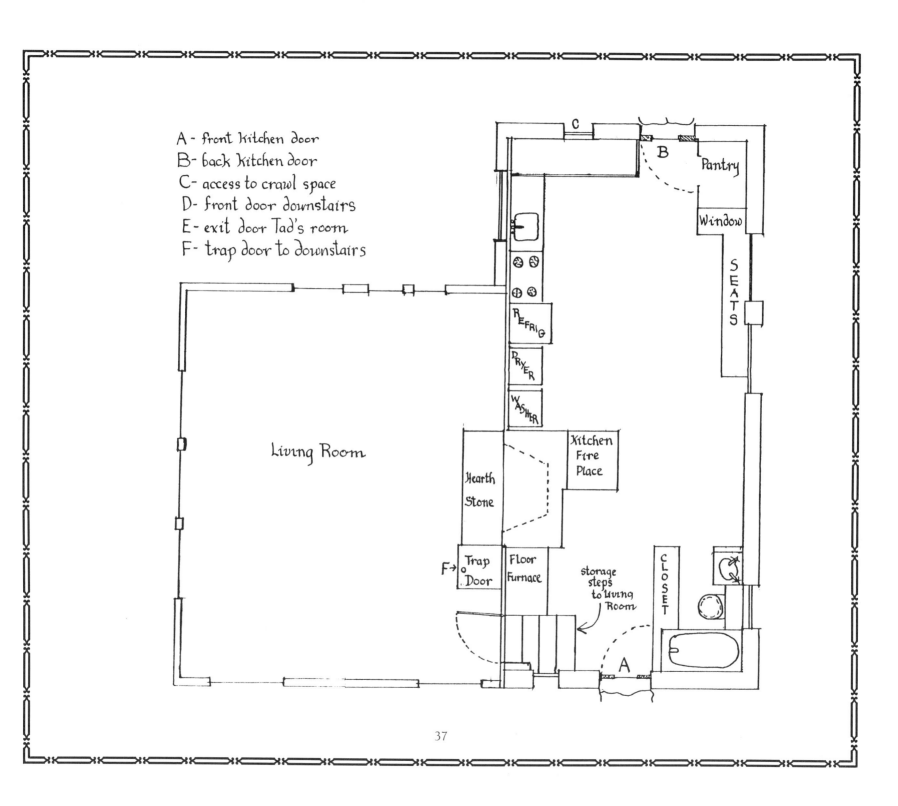

A - front kitchen door
B - back kitchen door
C - access to crawl space
D - front door downstairs
E - exit door Tad's room
F - trap door to downstairs

C

B

Pantry

Window

SEATS

Living Room

REFRIG

DRYER

WASHER

Kitchen Fire Place

Hearth Stone

F→ Trap Door

Floor Furnace

storage steps to living Room

CLOSET

A

# The Floor Plans

# of Our House

# Thinking Through the House

| what room | dimensions | ceiling height | door and frame dimensions | # windows | type window | source |
|-----------|-----------|----------------|---------------------------|-----------|-------------|--------|
|  |  |  |  |  |  |  |
|  |  |  |  |  |  |  |
|  |  |  |  |  |  |  |
|  |  |  |  |  |  |  |
|  |  |  |  |  |  |  |
|  |  |  |  |  |  |  |
|  |  |  |  |  |  |  |
|  |  |  |  |  |  |  |
|  |  |  |  |  |  |  |
|  |  |  |  |  |  |  |
|  |  |  |  |  |  |  |
|  |  |  |  |  |  |  |
|  |  |  |  |  |  |  |
|  |  |  |  |  |  |  |

# One Room at a Time

| list windows with dimensions/height from floor | storm window details | screen details | other notes |
| --- | --- | --- | --- |
| | | | |
| | | | |
| | | | |
| | | | |
| | | | |
| | | | |
| | | | |
| | | | |
| | | | |
| | | | |
| | | | |
| | | | |

# An Electrical Survey

Electricity should always be under the user's control. A great sense of security can be gained from knowing the source and hence how it can be turned off in emergency situations, most of which are, by definition, unexpected. The Case of Sylvia's Dog serves as an excellent example. Late one evening we heard several sharp reports from an adjacent room, which sounded like revolver shots. David entered to observe a hot, arcing short circuit in an old and very combustible cambric-covered light cord. Close examination, after disconnecting the lamp, revealed that the insulation was dried out and cracked. But why had it chosen this time to short out? Unattended, this small electrical fire could have destroyed the house. The answer was supplied by Sylvia's dog, Michelle. She was suffering an extended period of incontinence, brought about, in part, by one of her recurrent medical crises. It seems she had relieved herself on the wire, thereby supplying a conductive electrolyte between two separated wires that were uninsulated.

Somewhere inside your house there is a main breaker switch or a set of main fuses. These are analogous to a valve or water faucet and can be used to turn off the electricity coming into the house. In the case of fuses, the line side of the box is still hot when a fuse is pulled, so keep your hand away from the bared terminals. In many instances, the main fuse holders can be reversed and replaced in the off position, thereby shielding the line end. Usually the meter box is grounded, but in older installations, ground wires might have broken or clamps may rust through. David once witnessed a fire in an older house that was caused in part by the fact that the meter box was never grounded. Perhaps the meter readers had never noticed this condition, or if they had, they were not programmed to call it to the homeowner's attention. It is never a good idea to allow your house to be dependent upon the kindness of strangers.

For your wiring diagram you must locate the meter, and assure yourself that an armored wire is tightly connected to a ground stake or an uninterrupted metal water pipe leading underground.

Then find the main breaker or fuse holder. Now you can concern yourself with the branch circuits. In a house you are having built, you can have the electrician label the breaker switches and give you a wiring diagram of your house (these amenities aren't always volunteered). In older houses and, in particular, where there have been additions and extensions, it becomes more and more difficult to determine which fuses and breakers govern which outlets and appliances. One of the many reasons for this suggested exploration is so that you will not overload any given circuit. A toaster, a hair dryer, and an electric iron in simultaneous use will get you into the fuse-buying business in a hurry, or at least a trip to reset the circuit breaker.

Recently Sylvia gave one of our local appliance repairmen his modest minimum house-call charge of fifteen dollars for changing a fuse in an obscure box in her house. She had not even guessed its existence. Had the wiring diagram we are suggesting been available to us, she wouldn't be out the fifteen dollars.

It is customary for major electrical appliances, such as the submersible well pump, the clothes dryer, the kitchen stove, and the hot-water heater, to have individual circuits. Once these are labeled, it is time to search out the remainder of the electrical service. This is most easily accomplished in the daytime hours, and doing it with another person makes the work flow easily. Start with the refrigerator. With one of you peering at the light through a slightly open door, the breaker or fuse "technician" throws various breakers off, one at a time, until there is no power to the refrigerator, indicating that you have now located its circuit.

With a test light (which can be any lamp with a plug), the next step is to explore the area for other receptacles that are off. These will be on the same branch circuit as the refrigerator. Once each one is plotted, reactivate the circuit and repeat the process with each fuse or breaker.

An alternative method is to turn off the entire board and then reengage one circuit at a time, noting the various outlets controlled by that circuit. Of course while this is going on, be careful to plot receptacles that are controlled by their own wall switches, as well as switch-operated ceiling and outdoor lights.

If you are working alone, substitute a loud portable radio for the test light.

The electrical diagram of David's house follows.

You can color-code your circuits, individually, thereby achieving even greater clarity.

When the project is completed, remember to reset any electric clocks.

# Wiring Diagram

The four-outlet plug box behind the refrigerator is difficult to reach. The refrigerator, washing machine, gas stove, and an extension to the hi-fi system are plugged into it. The stove has its own outlet and a defunct electric clock. It also has a light with a switch. The bulb blew years ago, and David has never figured out how to replace it, having thoughtlessly discarded the directions that came with the stove. The switches for the overhead lights in the kitchen were installed before the kitchen table was in place, and now they require needless gymnastic effort. Blessed with hindsight, he now knows he should have put them on the wall of the pantry. Good sense would also have foreseen the need for a pantry light.

Once, before the well was drilled, there was a pump in the crawl space that brought water from a spring. It was removed, and the house has the luxury of an unused branch circuit.

David's breaker box, as illustrated by the diagram, is quite accessible. However, some fuse boxes are cleverly hidden, so you might want to include on the diagram a few hints for discovering yours.

Before undertaking more intrepid explorations of your house wiring, consult an experienced electrician.

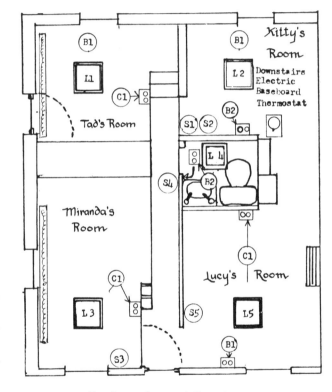

the downstairs children's rooms
are underneath the living room

44

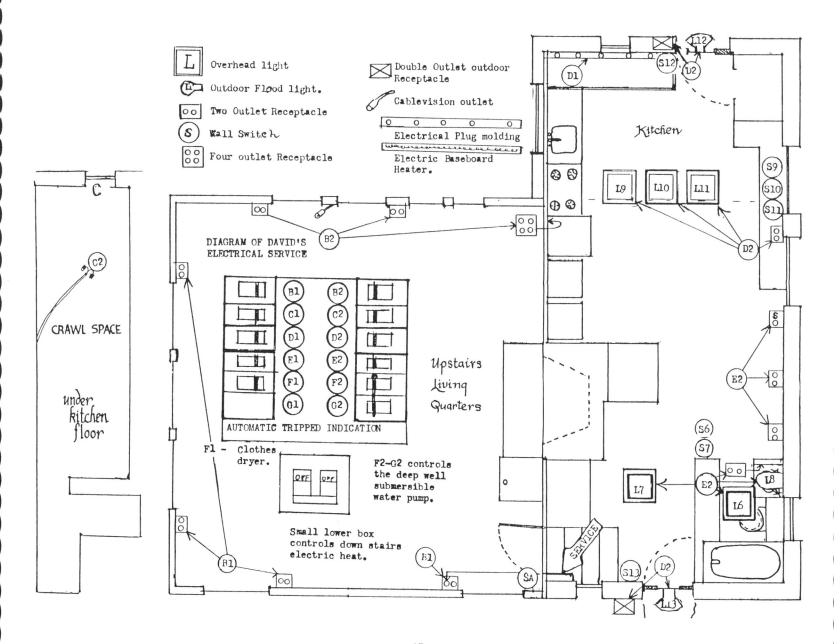

L  Overhead light

Outdoor Flood light.

Two Outlet Receptacle

S  Wall Switch

Four outlet Receptacle

Double Outlet outdoor Receptacle

Cablevision outlet

Electrical Plug molding

Electric Baseboard Heater.

Kitchen

CRAWL SPACE

under kitchen floor

DIAGRAM OF DAVID'S ELECTRICAL SERVICE

B1  B2
C1  C2
D1  D2
E1  E2
F1  F2
G1  G2

AUTOMATIC TRIPPED INDICATION

Upstairs Living Quarters

F1 – Clothes dryer.

F2–G2 controls the deep well submersible water pump.

OFF   OFF

Small lower box controls down stairs electric heat.

SERVICE

45

# Our Wiring Diagrams

# The House's Plumbing

There are many reasons for knowing where your house's plumbing is. Probably the best is so that you or any member of your family will know how to isolate aquatic disasters. Self-reliance isn't merely a money saver—professional help is not always available.

Outdoor plumbing can be indicated on the map of your adjacent grounds. Septic tank, drain fields, wellhead or spring, municipal water, or the hookup for a private water company should all be entered there. All the interior plumbing can be shown on a diagram of the house, which is a repeat of the basic floor plan. Pipes run up and down as well as back and forth, and sometimes it isn't easy to draw the water system. But even if you don't end up with a Mondrian painting, the avoidance of even just one aquatic disaster is well worth the trouble it takes to draw this diagram.

*IF YOU HAVE A WELL . . .*

Depth _____        Date drilled _____

Rate of flow _____        Dry spells or dates of limited delivery

Location _____        _____

Drilled by _____        Pump specifications _____
(Copy the specification plate. On deep-well submersibles this is best done prior to installation.)

Elbow  45° Elbow  Street Elbow  Tee  Cross  Lateral  Reducer  Close Nipple  Short Nipple  Cap  Bushing

Think of your house as a territory and the pipes as roads or canals running through it. To make a clear map, every pipe and valve should be found and charted. It is best to start at the point where the water supply enters the house. There is usually a pressure tank in the cellar or crawl space. One pipe leads into it from the water's source. All the rest of the plumbing is on the other, or house, side of this tank. If you have a municipal water supply, this starting point will usually be your water meter. It is also useful to remember that all hot-water lines lead back, in one way or another, to the water heater.

Code the hot- and cold-water pipes with different colors. Gas for the stove and oil for the furnace can also be included. Waste water and drainage can be yet another color.

You may have to poke around some to locate hidden water lines. If necessary, become a treasure hunter. Buy, borrow, or rent a metal locater. David once used one to find a wellhead that had been agonizingly lost. Of course any original plans for the house will put you way ahead, and strips of aluminum foil above buried plastic pipe will enable a metal detector to find it if necessary at some future date.

Drain plugs can be elusive. In colder climates, if you need to close the house, the plumbing must be turned off and drained. Some drain plugs are hidden from sight and must be located by feel. Sketches of these locations can be made, noting the dimensions of the plug shanks so that you will have the right wrench the first time, rather than having to go groping around in the dark with an assortment of inappropriate wrenches and skinned knuckles.

Which leads us to suggest that a most useful tool around the house is a droplight, which is a portable caged light bulb attached to a long electrical cord. Also note the shut-off valve or valves on your diagram and label their function. Once the plumbing format is familiar, you may want to consider making some changes. David, for example, plans to put shut-off valves on the pipes leading to his basement bathroom.

Maps and sketches can be crude if they are only to be reminders for the person who made them. We propose, however, that you make clear drawings that could be useful to a spouse, a tenant, or a house-sitter. These can also note specific curable difficulties. (In superfrigid weather there is one pipe in David's house that tends to freeze. A thermostatically controlled electric heat tape wrapped around it has resolved this problem.)

# Draining the House's Plumbing

David has reused the floor plan of his house, showing the adjacent children's rooms, while editing out the upstairs living room, which is devoid of plumbing. In the children's bathroom the pipes are buried in the floor slab and concealed in the west wall of Lucy's room. All the fixtures have isolating valves, and the specific drain plugs for this section of the system are located in the water-heater room.

As an aid to helping you design the proper sequence for turning off and draining the water in your house, here is how David explained the proper sequence to Sylvia, so that she could do it in an emergency or at least sensibly instruct a plumber to do it for her. As the various steps progress, you will see that certain aspects of the original plumbing system could have been more cleverly conceived.

Access to the crawl space is via the removable panel to the right of the back kitchen door as you face it from the outside. This panel is secured by two barrel bolts. With a flashlight or, better yet, the house's droplight plugged into the exterior outlet just to the right of this door, illuminate the interior.

(1) Shut down the valve on the incoming water line. Isolate the hot-water heater by turning off the cold-water intake valve (2). Turn the heater's gas supply off (3). Attach a hose to the faucet drain at the bottom of the hot-water heater (4). This hose must be long enough to lead out through the access opening and then down the hill for about twenty feet toward the dry well. Once started, it will then act as a siphon that will completely empty the hot-water tank. To facilitate the flow, open the hot-water faucets in the house. Remove the hose and allow any small residual water to drain into a pan that can then be dumped outside. Next attach the hose to the faucet drain on the cold-water pressure tank (5). Now you will be able to lead the drain hose further down the bank. The floor of this part of the crawl space is also below the level of the bottom of the access opening, and therefore the siphon effect is needed to empty this tank completely too. There are two drain plugs (6) over-

head, just before the entrance to the water-heater room. Unscrew these. Then unscrew the two drain plugs (7) from the lines leading to the downstairs bathroom. Most of the water in the pipes has been sucked back to the pressure tank and then out. The little that remains may be caught in a pan and then dumped outside. The two hoses (8) that come down from the washing machine need to be disconnected, and this finishes the final draining of the section of the water system that is contained in the crawl space.

Replacing the crawl space panel, we move up to the kitchen. There is a large sliding door just to the left of the front door as it is viewed from the inside. Face it and slide it to the left. Two drain plugs (9) are accessible near the front end of the bathtub. Remove these. Make sure that the shower is turned on so that the water in the pipe that leads up to the head can drain. Flush the upstairs toilet so as to empty the tank. Then sponge or pump out the remaining water in the bowl. Do the same for the downstairs toilet. Make sure that the outside faucet (10) is open. And finally the washing machine has to be pulled toward the center of the room so that its pump, held on by two large Phillips screws, can be removed and emptied. The drain hose from the washer can be lifted easily from its pipe so as to facilitate this movement.

Turning the water back on is essentially the reverse of this process. The toilets refill themselves.

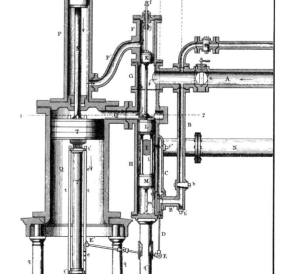

# by way of example
# the plumbing diagram of David's house

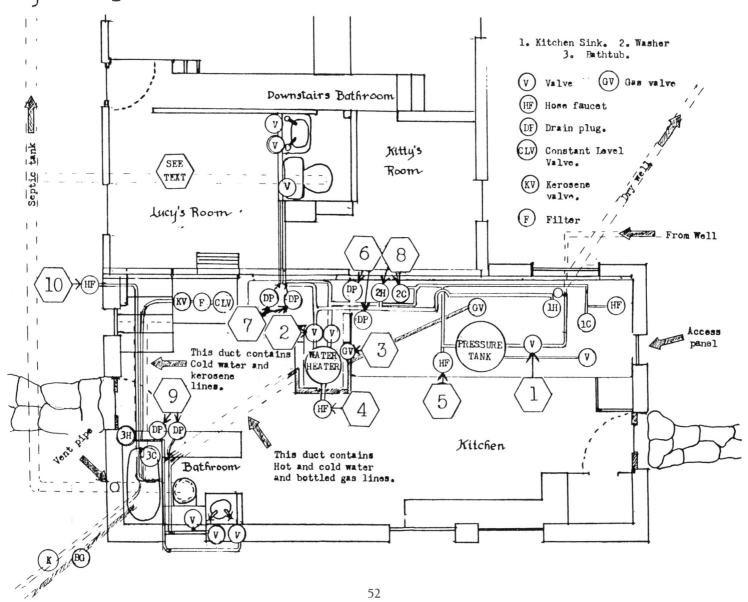

Downstairs Bathroom

Kitty's Room

1. Kitchen Sink.  2. Washer
3.  Bathtub.

(V)  Valve    (GV)  Gas valve

(HF)  Hose faucet

(DP)  Drain plug.

(CLV)  Constant Level Valve.

(KV)  Kerosene valve.

(F)  Filter

From Well

Dry Well

Lucy's Room

SEE TEXT

Septic tank

Vent pipe

Bathroom

This duct contains Cold water and kerosene lines.

This duct contains Hot and cold water and bottled gas lines.

WATER HEATER

PRESSURE TANK

Access panel

Kitchen

# The Diagram of Our Plumbing

# The Septic System

location of tank: _____

material of construction:_____

date of installation: _____

who installed: _____

capacity of tank: _____

_____

Record of Pumpings: _____

date                contractor              charge

_____

_____

_____

_____

_____ Treats for Your Septic System

_____

_____ sour milk

_____ brewer's yeast

Use this space for a diagram of your dry well and septic system

...five minutes after something is buried
it is as though it has been buried for-
ever if you don't mark it; include
written notes on location of drainfield
and tank – i.e.: directly in line with____
and ____ feet from_____.

# Roof Maintenance

| what roof | pitch | date | what was done | name, address, phone # of contractor | life expectancy |
|-----------|-------|------|---------------|--------------------------------------|-----------------|
|           |       |      |               |                                      |                 |
|           |       |      |               |                                      |                 |
|           |       |      |               |                                      |                 |
|           |       |      |               |                                      |                 |
|           |       |      |               |                                      |                 |
|           |       |      |               |                                      |                 |
|           |       |      |               |                                      |                 |
|           |       |      |               |                                      |                 |
|           |       |      |               |                                      |                 |
|           |       |      |               |                                      |                 |
|           |       |      |               |                                      |                 |
|           |       |      |               |                                      |                 |
|           |       |      |               |                                      |                 |
|           |       |      |               |                                      |                 |

note: leaks are very hard to find — the hole in the roof is not necessarily over the drip in the ceiling.

# Roofing Information

Especially when you've had *trouble* with a roofing situation, it is important to realize that different inclines (pitches) require different types of roofing. Be sure to get professional advice on the appropriate roofing for the area you wish to cover, bearing in mind that "professional advice" is not always perfect. Basic guidelines are usually written on the packaging.

With the advent of woodburning stoves, it's a good idea to use a shingle that is rated fireproof or fire-resistant.

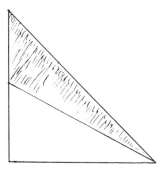

Flat to 1 in 12 Hot tar
Built-up membrane

1 in 12 to 3 in 12
Battle decking

3 in 12 to 6 in 12
Asphalt shingles

6 in 12 to 12 in 12 and
up Tile, wooden shingle
shakes, and slate

# The Heating System

type of fuel: _____

make of unit: _____ model number: _____ capacity: ___

where purchased: _____ price: _____

when purchased: _____

make of gun: _____ model number: _____

date of installation of unit: _____ who installed: _____

location of owner's manual: _____

location of maintenance contract: _____ service phone #: _____

location of filler pipe: _____

location of fuel tank: _____

name of fuel company that services us: _____

_____

Write a simple but complete explanation of how to re-start unit; carefully indicate location of switch; also diagram what the various valves are; know how to check whether there is fuel in the tank. Affix a copy of the explanation either here or near the unit in a clear plastic envelope.

# Helpful Hints

Consult with professionals about the advisability of having antifreeze added to the water-heating system. This would preclude frozen radiators and/or boilers in the event that the electric power should fail or you happen to run out of heating fuel. Some interior cold-water pipes in outside walls tend to freeze when outside temperatures fall below zero. One corrective mechanism is to install heat tapes, and sometimes it is helpful to open the cabinet doors beneath the kitchen sink.

# Details of Woodstoves

manufacturer : _____

model # or name: _____

where purchased : _____

price: _____

when purchased: _____

material of construction: _____

location of information regarding replacement parts: _____

who installed/when: _____

type of flue: _____

last replacement date: _____

optimal length wood: _____

length of firebox: _____

_____

_____

_____

_____

_____

# Helping Them Do Their Best

- furnace cement applied to cracks can make a cast iron stove more airtight; also asbestos cording covered with furnace cement can plug up leaks around doors.

- think about getting extra parts you know you'll need - so you won't be faced with their discontinuance.

# Details of Coal Stoves

manufacturer: _____

model # or name: _____

source: _____

purchase date: _____

price: _____

material of construction: _____

date of installation: _____

who installed: _____

type of flue: _____

last replacement date: _____

capacity: _____

length of burn: _____

_____

_____

_____

_____

# Keeping the Warmth In and The Cold Out or Vice Versa

Sylvia's favorite room was added to her house by the previous owner, whom we suspect was a cross between a polar bear and a fish, since there is no way of warming it and the ill-conceived flat roof began leaking within two years of its completion. The floors are so cold that three layers of rugs are necessary, and the crawl space underneath is so damp that we set a mousetrap there and caught a herring.

Once, years ago, in a desperate attempt to do something about this room, she hired someone to investigate what, if any, insulation was in the walls, floors, or ceiling. Whatever the findings were, the state of her finances at the time made her give up hope of remedying the situation, so she promptly forgot the diagnosis. We suggest that you keep track of whatever insulation information you discover.

| location | amount of insulation | type | notes |
|---|---|---|---|
|  |  |  |  |
|  |  |  |  |
|  |  |  |  |
|  |  |  |  |
|  |  |  |  |

# The Purchase of Appliances

If you get a new appliance, save the instruction book and put it in a safe and retrievable place. It is a useful guide and will instruct you in handling most minor emergencies. The older these booklets get, the more valuable they become. There are certain items that a new generation of repair people have never seen, let alone thought about. It is a good investment to replace missing manuals, if possible by writing to the company, or, failing that, you may be able to photocopy one owned by a friend. Due to the fact that he possesses the original manual for a vintage OC-3 Oliver crawler tractor, David is quite popular in a certain stratum of bulldozer society.

If possible, before purchasing a new appliance, make a trial run using a similar one at a friend or neighbor's house. Do you enjoy operating it? How much does it cost to run and do you find it comfortable to use?

On large appliances cost-account extra features. Weigh usefulness against price and monthly operating cost. Do you really need an icemaker in your life?

And now some minor thoughts on minor appliances: We are strongly encouraged in our consumer culture to buy numerous small machines, some of which turn out to be of dubious value. So, before turning to a Consumers Union report to pick out the best of whatever it is, decide whether you really want or need it in the first place. Have you considered the space it will consume versus the function it will serve?

Garage, cum yard, cum porch sales help reveal white elephants that run in packs. Electric knives and slicing machines seem to rival each other in their lack of usefulness, as witnessed by the fact that they abound at almost every sale. Should you persist in thinking that your electric knife will be different, give yourself a break and buy it or any object of current infatuation secondhand. Occasionally you can find something that you were about to buy anyway, something actually needed, but this is rare. David bought for two dollars a photocopying stand for his 35mm Minolta camera that he uses continually. "A much better buy" was an electric lawn mower that he has never used; however, "The cord alone is worth . . ."

Appliances that the owner is familiar with may fare poorly in unknowing hands. David once rented his house to a nice young couple who didn't know about cleaning the lint filter on a clothes dryer. He had assumed that everybody knew that lint filters were on dryers and that they needed regular cleanings. Like most assumptions, this one was wrong, and one day he returned to his house to find the tenants' clothes and the dryer in flames. Fortunately there was time to localize this disaster. In the owner's absence it is prudent to label major household appliances with proper usage instructions.

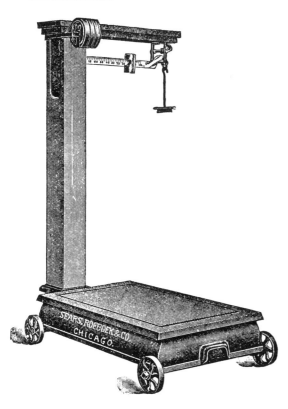

# Appliances

| appliance | purchase date | source | make & model # |
|---|---|---|---|
|  |  |  |  |
|  |  |  |  |
|  |  |  |  |
|  |  |  |  |
|  |  |  |  |
|  |  |  |  |
|  |  |  |  |
|  |  |  |  |
|  |  |  |  |
|  |  |  |  |
|  |  |  |  |
|  |  |  |  |
|  |  |  |  |
|  |  |  |  |

# Keeping Track of Them

| price | warrantee expires | location of owner's manual | location of service contract | name and phone # of service person |
|---|---|---|---|---|
| | | | | |
| | | | | |
| | | | | |
| | | | | |
| | | | | |
| | | | | |
| | | | | |
| | | | | |
| | | | | |
| | | | | |
| | | | | |
| | | | | |
| | | | | |
| | | | | |
| | | | | |
| | | | | |
| | | | | |

# The Wave of the Future

| what item | manufacturer | model number | serial number | date bought | cost |
|---|---|---|---|---|---|
|  |  |  |  |  |  |
|  |  |  |  |  |  |
|  |  |  |  |  |  |
|  |  |  |  |  |  |
|  |  |  |  |  |  |
|  |  |  |  |  |  |
|  |  |  |  |  |  |
|  |  |  |  |  |  |
|  |  |  |  |  |  |
|  |  |  |  |  |  |
|  |  |  |  |  |  |
|  |  |  |  |  |  |
|  |  |  |  |  |  |
|  |  |  |  |  |  |
|  |  |  |  |  |  |

# Electronics In Our Home

| warrantee information | care contract | information about hook-up, usage, care |
|---|---|---|
| | | |
| | | |
| | | |
| | | |
| | | |
| | | |
| | | |
| | | |
| | | |
| | | |
| | | |

# Recommended Items

Often we see some item that we might want to own ourselves, get for our house, or buy as a present for a friend. Like this book, for example, it may be a superior version of something we already have. This is the place to make a note of it against the day when the current one passes away.

| item | cost | where to purchase | who has one |
|------|------|-------------------|-------------|
|      |      |                   |             |
|      |      |                   |             |
|      |      |                   |             |
|      |      |                   |             |
|      |      |                   |             |
|      |      |                   |             |
|      |      |                   |             |
|      |      |                   |             |
|      |      |                   |             |
|      |      |                   |             |

| item | cost | where to purchase | who has one |
|------|------|-------------------|-------------|
|      |      |                   |             |
|      |      |                   |             |
|      |      |                   |             |
|      |      |                   |             |
|      |      |                   |             |
|      |      |                   |             |
|      |      |                   |             |
|      |      |                   |             |
|      |      |                   |             |
|      |      |                   |             |
|      |      |                   |             |
|      |      |                   |             |
|      |      |                   |             |

# Garages

construction date:_____

construction details:_____

_____

_____

if heated, details:_____

_____

_____

garage door:_____

_____

_____

driveway:_____

_____

_____

other:_____

_____

_____

# Other Out Buildings

*Building:* _____

_____

_____

_____

_____

_____

*Building:* _____

_____

_____

_____

_____

_____

_____

# Swimming Pools

This is, by necessity, a very open page. In Kansas we might be looking at a stock tank and a windmill, in drier places maybe just a birdbath that is only half-filled. You might have a lake, a pond, or even a spring on your property, or be near the ocean or a stream. Do you have a dock, a dam, or a waterwheel? Have you ever successfully stocked some appropriate species of fish? And are you aware that in many jurisdictions it is illegal to release goldfish into public waters?

date built or purchased: _____

contractor or manufacturer: _____

capacity: _____

make of pump: _____

make of filter: _____

dimensions: _____

model # of pump: _____

model # of filter: _____

_____

location of pool maintenance schedule: _____

required chemicals and their sources: _____

# Other Aquatic Environments

Weirs: _____

_____

Floating Docks: _____

_____

Moorings: _____

_____

Water Wheels: _____

_____

Lakes and Ponds: _____

_____

Springs and their maintenance: _____

_____

Fish that have been stocked and when: ____

_____

_____

# Zoning Ordinances and Building Codes

In rural areas building codes haven't been around all that long, and you can skip this page if you live in a place that doesn't have them. Until recently it was assumed that the law of gravity was the only building code one needed and that anyone who violated it too rashly would perish in his own structure's collapse, thereby accomplishing a laudatory decrease in the population of imbeciles. For many reasons, all that has changed. We are suggesting here that, before you build, you note down specific rules and regulations that apply to you. Also note where the full text of your local ordinances can be found (usually in the town clerk's office) and what, if any, variances have been permitted. Usually a building permit is required before you can do almost anything.

A lot of zoning was brought about by the fact that winds are changeable and hogs aren't lilac bushes.

One of our nearby neighbors got somewhat carried away while constructing a studio around a huge dead oak tree. He went over the township's prescribed height limit, and his structure was slated to be demolished until someone discovered that all the nearby neighbors had become quite fond of it, and unless someone knew exactly where to look, it was not readily visible. As zoning develops in your community, it isn't a bad idea to show some interest in it, because you may feel that your input is more or equally as rational as whoever is taking the trouble to make up community rules you will have to live by.

Research potential projects. For example, can you convert your unused two-car garage into a rentable flat?

# Applicable Zoning Rules

minimum permitted acreage per dwelling:_____

maximum building height:_____

minimum distance from building to boundary line:_____

number of derelict vehicles permitted:_____

number of allowable occupants:_____

prohibited livestock:_____

other:_____

_____

_____

_____

_____

_____

_____

_____

phone # local building inspector:_____

phone # local Board of Fire Underwriters' representative:_____

# Alterations and Additions

| what change | date | who did the job-name, address, phone# |
| --- | --- | --- |
|  |  |  |
|  |  |  |
|  |  |  |
|  |  |  |
|  |  |  |
|  |  |  |
|  |  |  |
|  |  |  |
|  |  |  |
|  |  |  |
|  |  |  |
|  |  |  |
|  |  |  |

# We Have Made

| cost | building permit details | maintenance instructions | notes |
|------|------------------------|-------------------------|-------|
|      |                        |                         |       |
|      |                        |                         |       |
|      |                        |                         |       |
|      |                        |                         |       |
|      |                        |                         |       |
|      |                        |                         |       |
|      |                        |                         |       |
|      |                        |                         |       |
|      |                        |                         |       |
|      |                        |                         |       |
|      |                        |                         |       |
|      |                        |                         |       |
|      |                        |                         |       |

# The Future of Our House

more changes we might make

An envelope to hold
hints, arrangements
and ideas
that have caught our fancy.

SURFACES

# Painting the Interior

| date | what was painted | type of paint | brand of paint | color # and name | primer? |
|------|------------------|---------------|----------------|------------------|---------|
|      |                  |               |                |                  |         |
|      |                  |               |                |                  |         |
|      |                  |               |                |                  |         |
|      |                  |               |                |                  |         |
|      |                  |               |                |                  |         |
|      |                  |               |                |                  |         |
|      |                  |               |                |                  |         |
|      |                  |               |                |                  |         |
|      |                  |               |                |                  |         |
|      |                  |               |                |                  |         |
|      |                  |               |                |                  |         |
|      |                  |               |                |                  |         |
|      |                  |               |                |                  |         |
|      |                  |               |                |                  |         |
|      |                  |               |                |                  |         |

# of Our House

| #coats | #gal. used | who painted | #hrs. | cost | location of leftover paint | color swatch |
|--------|-----------|-------------|-------|------|---------------------------|--------------|
|        |           |             |       |      |                           |              |
|        |           |             |       |      |                           |              |
|        |           |             |       |      |                           |              |
|        |           |             |       |      |                           |              |
|        |           |             |       |      |                           |              |
|        |           |             |       |      |                           |              |
|        |           |             |       |      |                           |              |
|        |           |             |       |      |                           |              |
|        |           |             |       |      |                           |              |
|        |           |             |       |      |                           |              |
|        |           |             |       |      |                           |              |
|        |           |             |       |      |                           |              |
|        |           |             |       |      |                           |              |
|        |           |             |       |      |                           |              |

# Painting the Exterior

| date | what was painted | type of paint | brand of paint | color # and name | primer? |
|------|------------------|---------------|----------------|------------------|---------|
|      |                  |               |                |                  |         |
|      |                  |               |                |                  |         |
|      |                  |               |                |                  |         |
|      |                  |               |                |                  |         |
|      |                  |               |                |                  |         |
|      |                  |               |                |                  |         |
|      |                  |               |                |                  |         |
|      |                  |               |                |                  |         |
|      |                  |               |                |                  |         |
|      |                  |               |                |                  |         |
|      |                  |               |                |                  |         |
|      |                  |               |                |                  |         |
|      |                  |               |                |                  |         |

# of Our House

| #coats | #gal. used | who painted | #hrs. | cost | location of leftover paint | color swatch |
|--------|-----------|-------------|-------|------|---------------------------|--------------|
|        |           |             |       |      |                           |              |
|        |           |             |       |      |                           |              |
|        |           |             |       |      |                           |              |
|        |           |             |       |      |                           |              |
|        |           |             |       |      |                           |              |
|        |           |             |       |      |                           |              |
|        |           |             |       |      |                           |              |
|        |           |             |       |      |                           |              |
|        |           |             |       |      |                           |              |
|        |           |             |       |      |                           |              |
|        |           |             |       |      |                           |              |
|        |           |             |       |      |                           |              |
|        |           |             |       |      |                           |              |
|        |           |             |       |      |                           |              |

# Floors

| floor | covering details-i.e. manufacturer, style #, amount or size | purchased at |
| --- | --- | --- |
| | | |
| | | |
| | | |
| | | |
| | | |
| | | |
| | | |
| | | |
| | | |
| | | |
| | | |
| | | |
| | | |

Note: Very often the best floor care is the least costly . . .

# And Floor Coverings

| date | cost | recommended care | other notes |
|------|------|------------------|-------------|
|      |      |                  |             |
|      |      |                  |             |
|      |      |                  |             |
|      |      |                  |             |
|      |      |                  |             |
|      |      |                  |             |
|      |      |                  |             |
|      |      |                  |             |
|      |      |                  |             |
|      |      |                  |             |
|      |      |                  |             |

taking off shoes upon entering house

# Walls

| wall(s) | what coverings - including details | where purchased |
|---------|-----------------------------------|-----------------|
|         |                                   |                 |
|         |                                   |                 |
|         |                                   |                 |
|         |                                   |                 |
|         |                                   |                 |
|         |                                   |                 |
|         |                                   |                 |
|         |                                   |                 |
|         |                                   |                 |
|         |                                   |                 |
|         |                                   |                 |
|         |                                   |                 |

# And Wall Coverings

| when | cost | recommended care | other notes |
|------|------|------------------|-------------|
|      |      |                  |             |
|      |      |                  |             |
|      |      |                  |             |
|      |      |                  |             |
|      |      |                  |             |
|      |      |                  |             |
|      |      |                  |             |
|      |      |                  |             |
|      |      |                  |             |
|      |      |                  |             |
|      |      |                  |             |
|      |      |                  |             |
|      |      |                  |             |
|      |      |                  |             |

# Wall Coverings We Have Used

...with name, style number,
manufacturer, source, cost
noted on reverse side...

# MAINTENANCE

# Security

Your home's most effective security device is the hand of an honest man. Most household locks are only meant to keep out friends. However, secure locks and stout doors delay forcible entry, long enough either for you to phone for police assistance or for you to make a retreat, which is the first prerequisite of a legal self-defense.

Keys have magical significance. Children grow up on fairy tales about wondrous and horrible places that one needs keys to enter—ogre's castles, magic treasure chests, and enchanted gardens. Keys to the city, keys to the kingdom, these all symbolize love, power, and trust. A friend gives you the key to his house in the country or to his apartment in the city. Keys are opportunities, and the more keys you have that fit things, the more opportunities you possess. Keys give access and maintain exclusiveness—*but* only if they fit something. All of us seem to have a collection of useless keys that don't fit anything, and there is certainly nothing deader than an old key. We seem to have trouble getting rid of them, largely because we don't really know if they are old keys or not. Sylvia has a huge bowl containing hundreds of them. In it we found the original real estate agent's key to her house. It was tagged with the previous owner's name and the house's purchase price. That was it. All others seem to be unidentifiable orphans. Still, she is reluctant to discard them. The only sure throwaways are old car keys for various makes of cars clearly no longer owned.

This brings us to the key board, where you may wish to store your original car, motorcycle, file cabinet, attaché case, and desk or bureau keys. This board can be as simple as some nails driven into the inside of a wooden cabinet door, or it can be a shallow cabinet with a door and lock of its own. There is a tendency for duplicate keys to be made from whatever is most readily available, so we often wind up getting copies of copies, and numerous slight errors multiply, until we are confronted with the curse of the cranky key. If copies are made from the originals, no error gets introduced. Try newly made keys as soon as they are obtained.

*IDENTIFICATION*   One can label master keys with little round cardboard tags. It is also possible to obtain a set of letter stamps with which to mark the function of the key. The key to the front door of my house is depicted here. You can also use a **V** file to notch keys that are often used in the dark. If you always notch the key's upper edge, you won't have to blunder about trying wrong keys in upside-down insertions. And if you want to differentiate keys, use one notch for the front door, two for the back, and on to the next most used.

If you have combinations for locks, it is a good idea to write them down. How about your post office box when you have asked a friend to pick up the mail? You know how it works through dint of long practice, but sometimes a combination is difficult to describe in words. This may call for a sketch.

Odd keys can be visually verified against the master board and, if they look right, can be tried in the appropriate lock. If they do not work, then dispose of them in some manner that will not do violence to your sense of magic.

Incidentally, the more sophisticated your set of locks, the greater the need for you to have keys for them. The friendly old-fashioned spring-loaded bolt lock, which can be forced open with the blade of a kitchen knife, is the key loser's friend. Now try a Fox Police Lock. You need either the specific key or several sticks of dynamite.

One practical-minded friend suggested that in a new house the external locks be identical, so that one key fits them all. And how about designating a specific peg for car keys, to avoid misplacing them? You may want to think out a proper sequence for locking up your house. How about the location of any hidden keys? And where is a tool that can open the bathroom door after a small child has locked himself inside? And of course, the house should always have its own mailbox key if one is needed.

We haven't done much with locks. As it is in many houses, tiny bolts go into thin tin mortises attached to pieces of flimsy trim. This means that if anyone were seriously trying to get in, the door would serve briefly as a noise maker.

Before deciding on the lock you want, consider your neighborhood, your lifestyle and how much money it will cost to keep your peace of mind. A dog might be more enjoyable and effective than a $2000 alarm system. David has a dog watching his place when he's away, but it's hard to tell how much a watch dog watches when you're not watching it. However, when the snow melted several springs ago, there was a pry bar near his front door, and beside it a boot.

# The Keys to Our Kingdom

| location of lock | make | type | key # | where purchased | location of extra keys |
|---|---|---|---|---|---|
| | | | | | |
| | | | | | |
| | | | | | |
| | | | | | |
| | | | | | |
| | | | | | |
| | | | | | |
| | | | | | |
| | | | | | |
| | | | | | |
| | | | | | |
| | | | | | |
| | | | | | |
| | | | | | |

# Alarm System Details

With the alarm system in place, a clear, step-by-step sequence that everybody in the house understands is probably the best way of maintaining both your possessions and your sanity.

Make of system.

Who services it.

Police jurisdiction responding to a central ringer.

_____

_____

_____

_____

_____

_____

_____

_____

# Preparing the House to be Unoccupied

Whenever the house is left, even for a few days and especially during the winter, it is wise to turn off the entering water. This involves either turning off the power to the pump if there is a well or shutting off a valve if the house is on city or town water. Thus, should there be a plumbing failure, flooding will be limited to the volume of water contained in the isolated system. Indicate the location of these valves and switches on your plumbing and electrical diagrams.

For an absence of a few days you may not want to turn off the hot-water heater, or again you may. Sylvia's electric hot-water heater is easily turned on and off. David's bottled-gas one requires a goodly amount of effort, both to shut down and to relight.

Of course, if you are going to turn off the heat and close the house in winter, then all pipes and all storage tanks must be drained. Washing machines and dishwashers need attending to. David's washing machine has a pump on the back that needs to be removed so that residual water doesn't freeze and ruin it. One of the luxuries his house enjoys is patented freeze-proof traps beneath all the drains. Most traps aren't freeze-proof and must be emptied when the house is closed. These traps have two functions: They maintain a column of water that prevents gas formed in the sewer system from getting back into the house and they catch and retain any valuable items that fall into the drains.

If you are going away for only a few days, a house watcher can be very helpful. One way to make his or her efforts more successful is to get a thermal switch that turns on a clearly visible light at, say 40 degrees Fahrenheit, alerting this custodian to the fact that trouble is in the wings and help is needed fast. For security, you of course don't want to have newspaper and milk deliveries mounting up on your stoop. And consider various time-programmed switches that turn lights on and off around the house even when no one is home. Telephone service can also be suspended and your calls referred to another number, often for nearly the same cost as having the phone disconnected and then reconnected.

# Providing For Care

To Be Notified: _____

    local police station: _____

    concerned neighbors: _____

_____

possible house sitters: _____

_____

does house sitter know phone number of: _____

    plumber: _____

    roofer: _____

    furnace maintenance: _____

    where we can be reached: _____

    snow plow person: _____

_____

and for the short haul: _____

    someone who will come and feed our pets: _____

_____

    someone to water our plants: _____

# When We're Not There

Consider Turning Off: _____

    fuel oil: _____    gas: _____

    water: _____    refrigerator: _____

    electricity: _____    telephone: _____

_____

deliveries to be stopped: _____

_____

_____

and for the long haul: _____

people who will board our pets: _____

or a place that will board our pets: _____

check in and check out times: _____   rates: _____

_____

_____

people who will board our tropical fish: _____

people who will board our plants: _____

other: _____

# Maintenance

As the seasons come and go, predictable chores, if anticipated, can be simplified. There is no need to be surprised each autumn when the leaves decide to die. And if you are careless and leave your outdoor tools around, the first fallen snow magically transforms your yard into a treasure hunt. Are there heat tapes for your gutters, and where are canvas awnings stored?

*THE HOUSE*  Maybe a day to polish silver, or restore tranquillity to the attic? A leaky-faucet day or one for gutter cleaning? How about wooden-furniture repair or even an antirust crusade? Maybe this year oil the bearings on the weather vane. Christmas ornaments are best repaired and cleaned as they are being put away.

*THE LAND*  Clean birdhouse; prepare to tap the sugar maple trees. Prune the apple or the avocado and gather up dry kindling. Wash the cider press and maybe catch some worms before the fishing season starts. Refurbish signs, brighten crèches, straighten fences, and scold the squirrels when they plunder food intended for the birds.

# Thoughts On Time and Motion

Often, due to the fact that no one in the family actually knows how long a job takes, doing it or even contemplating doing it engenders a great deal of contention. If we are certain that, on the average, it requires four minutes and thirty seconds to take out the garbage, then, even if a member of the family wants a wound stripe for each mission, he knows that he can't rightly put in for a medal.

Accomplishments prosper on a diet of human hours. The bigger the lawn the more of them it will eat. We once met a lady who was looking harried. She was in a new house in the country and was rapidly running out of time. She had never figured out the number of hours needed for each specific job and had undertaken many more projects than she had time for. Knowing how much one is doing is the first step toward a proper pace and an even gait. Harried work tires you two and a half times faster than work that is restfully scheduled. Don't bite off more than you can chew.

Feeding the horse, bathing the dog, or pruning an apple tree and also picking up the cut branches afterward? Shoveling snow off the walks, or cleaning leaves from out of the gutters? Changing a washer in the sink, or washing and waxing the car? Feeding the tropical fish, the cat, the canary? And how about cleaning the parakeet's cage? Washing the family's dinner dishes, digging worms for a fishing trip (this should be done the day before), or thoroughly cleaning the swimming pool? Replacing a sledgehammer handle? Finding a splitting wedge that's been lost in the snow? Vacuuming the living room, or removing skid marks from a toilet bowl? Refinishing a chest of drawers, or rewiring a lamp? Newly making a bed as opposed to merely reenlisting it? Really washing a bathtub? Cleaning, peeling, and canning twenty quarts of peaches, or picking a pint of wild strawberries?

# The Work Force

| name of employee | address | phone | recommended by |
| --- | --- | --- | --- |
|  |  |  |  |
|  |  |  |  |
|  |  |  |  |
|  |  |  |  |
|  |  |  |  |
|  |  |  |  |
|  |  |  |  |
|  |  |  |  |
|  |  |  |  |
|  |  |  |  |
|  |  |  |  |
|  |  |  |  |
|  |  |  |  |

# of Our House

| job done | remuneration | dates of employment | notes |
|---|---|---|---|
| | | | |
| | | | |
| | | | |
| | | | |
| | | | |
| | | | |
| | | | |
| | | | |
| | | | |
| | | | |
| | | | |
| | | | |
| | | | |

# Replaceable Maintenance Items

Certain things must be continually replaced in order for a house to remain operational. Running out of something often entails running out to buy it. Even more irritating than having run out of something you need is getting it and finding it's the wrong thing or the wrong size. This usually happens on a Sunday or after the stores are closed. It is always useful to note down specific nomenclatures. The surest way to match the crushed stone or gravel in your driveway is to make a note of its official size. And sink washers never fail until they know that their type and size are long forgotten. Gaffer's tape, nylon net twine, a well-organized assortment of different-size nails, black electrician's tape, wood glue, picture hangers, phonograph needles, specific light bulbs, and any other of the small artifacts that have caused inconvenience by their absence in the past—whatever you have that you may need to replace, here's the space to make a note of its specifications:

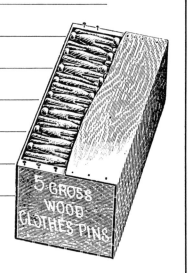

# Instructions For Simple Maintenance

*periodic chores made easy*

Once you have learned to do something, keep a record of how. Attach an envelope to this page which will contain cards with written explanations and diagrams; i.e. how to change the washer in the kitchen sink. or how you once gained access to seemingly inaccessible places.

# A Log of All Repairs

| date | what system | nature of repair | name, address, phone # of contractor |
|------|-------------|------------------|--------------------------------------|
|      |             |                  |                                      |
|      |             |                  |                                      |
|      |             |                  |                                      |
|      |             |                  |                                      |
|      |             |                  |                                      |
|      |             |                  |                                      |
|      |             |                  |                                      |
|      |             |                  |                                      |
|      |             |                  |                                      |
|      |             |                  |                                      |
|      |             |                  |                                      |
|      |             |                  |                                      |
|      |             |                  |                                      |
|      |             |                  |                                      |
|      |             |                  |                                      |
|      |             |                  |                                      |
|      |             |                  |                                      |

# To Household Systems

| cost | guarantee | evaluation of work | notes |
|------|-----------|--------------------|-------|
|      |           |                    |       |
|      |           |                    |       |
|      |           |                    |       |
|      |           |                    |       |
|      |           |                    |       |
|      |           |                    |       |
|      |           |                    |       |
|      |           |                    |       |
|      |           |                    |       |
|      |           |                    |       |
|      |           |                    |       |
|      |           |                    |       |
|      |           |                    |       |
|      |           |                    |       |
|      |           |                    |       |

# A Log of All Repairs

| date | what appliance | what repair | cost |
|---|---|---|---|
|  |  |  |  |
|  |  |  |  |
|  |  |  |  |
|  |  |  |  |
|  |  |  |  |
|  |  |  |  |
|  |  |  |  |
|  |  |  |  |
|  |  |  |  |
|  |  |  |  |
|  |  |  |  |
|  |  |  |  |
|  |  |  |  |

# To Household Appliances

| name and phone # of repair person | what caused the breakdown /other |
|---|---|
| | |
| | |
| | |
| | |
| | |
| | |
| | |
| | |
| | |
| | |
| | |
| | |
| | |

# A Log of All Repairs

| date | what item | what repair |
|------|-----------|-------------|
|      |           |             |
|      |           |             |
|      |           |             |
|      |           |             |
|      |           |             |
|      |           |             |
|      |           |             |
|      |           |             |
|      |           |             |
|      |           |             |
|      |           |             |
|      |           |             |
|      |           |             |
|      |           |             |

# To Electronics In Our House

| guarantee? | name and phone# of repair person | cause of damage |
|---|---|---|
| | | |
| | | |
| | | |
| | | |
| | | |
| | | |
| | | |
| | | |
| | | |
| | | |
| | | |

# Projects in the Wings

David keeps a list of things he wants to do, which he checks off and dates as the various projects are accomplished. As the years pass, surprising numbers of them get done. Looking at the projects checked off and completed serves to raise a banner against the sense of futility and sloth. Somewhere near the beginning of the list is a restoration project that hasn't been gotten to as yet. It is a fine antique German Jaeger rifle purchased from Ed Agranonte for eight dollars in 1954.

To avoid endlessly running to town or even just around the corner, and because hardware stores are often closed on Sundays, our friend, Tom Beecham's method of project accomplishment is to get all the needed materials and tools placed in close proximity to the job at hand. Then he begins. We might call this facilitation through preparedness.

# Things To Be Done

# Dealing With

Household pests come in all sizes and shapes. Flying squirrels in the attic can savage insulation and keep the human inhabitants awake. Wood-peckers can launch a jack-hammerlike attack against a house's siding. Ants invade the sugar, and silverfish eat up the books. In spring, sleeping wasps awaken to invade.

From a flat surface any bug can be safely returned to the outdoors. Cover it with an inverted glass, then slide an in-dex card between the mouth of the glass and the surface the bug is on, thus effecting cap-ture. If you want to kill mice, use thread to tie the bait to the trigger of the trap. If you just want to run a combination mouse feeder and intelligence test, eliminate the thread.

| pest | date | location | cause, if known |
|------|------|----------|-----------------|
|  |  |  |  |
|  |  |  |  |
|  |  |  |  |
|  |  |  |  |
|  |  |  |  |
|  |  |  |  |
|  |  |  |  |
|  |  |  |  |
|  |  |  |  |
|  |  |  |  |
|  |  |  |  |
|  |  |  |  |
|  |  |  |  |
|  |  |  |  |
|  |  |  |  |

# Household Pests

| remedy | instructions | safety precautions | recommended frequency |
|--------|--------------|--------------------|-----------------------|
|        |              |                    |                       |
|        |              |                    |                       |
|        |              |                    |                       |
|        |              |                    |                       |
|        |              |                    |                       |
|        |              |                    |                       |
|        |              |                    |                       |
|        |              |                    |                       |
|        |              |                    |                       |
|        |              |                    |                       |
|        |              |                    |                       |
|        |              |                    |                       |

# A Record

| date | nature of pest | location | chemical used |
|------|----------------|----------|---------------|
|      |                |          |               |
|      |                |          |               |
|      |                |          |               |
|      |                |          |               |
|      |                |          |               |
|      |                |          |               |
|      |                |          |               |
|      |                |          |               |
|      |                |          |               |
|      |                |          |               |
|      |                |          |               |
|      |                |          |               |
|      |                |          |               |
|      |                |          |               |

# of Professional Exterminations

| effectiveness | exterminator's name and phone no. | guarantee, if any |
|---|---|---|
|  |  |  |
|  |  |  |
|  |  |  |
|  |  |  |
|  |  |  |
|  |  |  |
|  |  |  |
|  |  |  |
|  |  |  |
|  |  |  |
|  |  |  |
|  |  |  |
|  |  |  |

# Firefighting Equipment

Most house fires have small and extinguishable beginnings, and if you are there with proper equipment, catastrophe can be averted.

David's house has a specific hose attached to its own faucet inside the cabinet beneath the kitchen sink. It is carefully coiled and not buried under a welter of cleaning materials or bundled-up rags. And, most important, it is permanently there. It does not get borrowed so as to extend garden hoses or to wash cars. It is the house's very own. Its position near the back kitchen door makes for availability against both brush and chimney fires. There is an outside hydrant near the front door, and this has its own hose during all the frost-free months. In summer there is an additional hydrant outside the back kitchen door. Whenever he connects a hose, he looks very carefully to see that the washer is in place.

A can of baking soda near a kitchen stove is handy against minor cooking-fat fires. Almost every restaurant fire you hear about starts in the exhaust ducts over the stove, because no one has been given the job of periodically cleaning them and everyone spends his time wondering whose job it is, right up until the very moment that the restaurant burns down.

It's ten o'clock at night. Do you know where your fire extinguishers are? David's house has two. One is a five-pound $CO_2$, and the other is a five-pound dry chemical. Both are in working order, recently weighed and inspected. Sometimes a local fire department will service them, or you can look up "Fire Extinguishers" in the Yellow Pages. Here is as good a place as any to write down the phone numbers, although hopefully they are also on the extinguisher's inspection tag. Does everyone in the house know where the extinguishers are and how they operate? Of course, once used, they have to be recharged. A fire extinguisher is one of the nicest presents you can buy the house. We acknowledge that good ones are expensive, but one costs approximately what a meal for two with drinks would come to in a medium-priced restaurant nowadays. Your house protects you from the elements, and you in turn should protect your house.

# General Safety Rules

On March 25, 1911, 145 lives were lost in the Triangle Shirt Company fire. There is also a little child's grave in Wilson, Connecticut, containing the body of a clearly identifiable little blue-eyed blonde who died in the Ringling Brothers Circus fire of 1944. Her body was never claimed. As a tribute to the many lives that have been uselessly and tragically lost in avoidable conflagrations, we suggest the following guidelines for dealing with fire:

*AVOIDANCE*   A stove or a furnace is a mechanism for maintaining and isolating a very hot fire from the rest of your house. Tin rusts, bricks decay, and soot accumulates, so inspection and maintenance must be continual, and the furnace area should always be kept clear of combustibles. Common danger spots are chimneys, flues, and defective fireplaces. Make certain your installations meet or exceed the Board of Fire Underwriters' code. With a woodstove—even if you've done everything properly—monitor the system for a while before leaving it untended. Feel the area around the pipes, and make sure that adjacent materials aren't being heated nearly to the point of combustion. Probably a good rule is, if you can't hold your hand on comfortably, it's too hot.

Certain older installations were never meant to be for real. A fireplace in a lovely old brick city home seemed to contain a cheery blaze on Christmas Eve, but on Christmas morning the fire engines arrived with alacrity. Tragedy was averted. The firemen explained that these particular decorative fireplaces were designed to hold only the small ceramic gas log long-past generations once used to underheat Victorian sitting rooms.

Sylvia says that everybody knows about children and matches, but everybody obviously doesn't, or there would be far fewer disasters involving them. Smoking in bed is a way that many smokers have successfully avoided lung cancer's more lingering death.

*DISCOVERY*   If you are awake, or awakened, a very fine smoke detector is your own nose. If you smell smoke, it is always from something. Make certain of the source. David's father once woke up in the middle of the night because he smelled a burning house nearly two miles away before the people inside it did. Trust your nose. Sylvia smelled something wrong in her kitchen. She would not be dissuaded by a careful inspection that revealed nothing. It was finally discovered that there was a low-level short circuit in a receptacle, which, if unattended, had the potential to burn the house down. In addition to being reasonably priced, smoke and heat alarms are mandated for most new construction.

*ESCAPING*   Plan and practice various fire escape routes and drill your family on them. Designated assembly points safely distant from the house will enable you to know that everyone has been successfully evacuated. If the house is large and your family numerous, you may want to establish a buddy system. Make sure that all the windows you are counting on as exits open freely. Someday you might want to go to the town dump and find some old windows so that you can teach yourself and your children how to smash them out with a chair (while of course facing away from them so as to protect your eyes). A friend's wife was vacationing in Maine, staying in a huge old farmhouse. A fire started, and in minutes the building was engulfed in flames. Fortunately everyone escaped with their lives, and now she has a commercially manufactured emergency fire ladder in the second-floor bedroom of her home. Never return to a burning building except to make a qualified attempt to save a human life. If there is an older person left alone in the house, we implore you to have an organized plan of rescue that can also be imparted, we would hope, to neighbors. A freon-powered portable boat horn can be used to attract attention. Baby-sitters should be familiar with your fire evacuation plan. In fact, always be aware of the possibility of fire and preplan your escape from any building you may be in.

*FIGHTING*   As already mentioned, you are not the fire department and cannot deal with major conflagrations. However, David once successfully fought down a well-started fire in a New York City loft. A pile of newspapers had stupidly been permitted to accumulate next to a fireplace. A bucket brigade from the kitchen finally doused the flames, and it was only then that, fortunately for the fish, David noticed a thirty-gallon fish tank that had been adjacent to the blaze. In the country a rake, shovel, or wet broom, vigorously wielded, can successfully contain small-scale grass fires. Here is a place to write your own fire regulations.

*THE SPECIFIC FIRE REGULATIONS OF OUR HOUSE*

Never leave a room that contains a fire in a fireplace without making sure that the firescreen is placed in front of it.

If you can't comfortably touch the remains of an outdoor fire, don't ever leave it.

# Our Fire Drill Plan

# A List of Firefighting and Detection Equipment

| item: | location: | recommended service schedule: | most recent inspection: |
|---|---|---|---|
|  |  |  |  |
|  |  |  |  |
|  |  |  |  |
|  |  |  |  |
|  |  |  |  |
|  |  |  |  |
|  |  |  |  |
|  |  |  |  |
|  |  |  |  |

Make note of special conditions. In times of drought the forests here are closed to hunters and campers:

# Emergencies Other Than Fire

*POWER FAILURES*   For secondary illumination, have on hand a sufficient supply of candles and whatever form of kerosene-, propane-, or battery-powered lanterns you feel most comfortable with. Cyalume lightsticks are inert until flexed, when they emit a source of safe light akin to the presence of a huge firefly. It isn't a bright light, but it is useful if you're searching for others or as a beacon. These have a limited shelf life and should be periodically replaced.

David treats an emergency flashlight as though his life or someone else's depended on it, because it well might. It is always kept in one specific place, is magnetic, and clings to a steel plate handy to his bed. For a few extra bucks, small, plug-in, night-lights are available. These contain rechargeable cadmium batteries. Plugged into any 110-volt AC wall socket, they automatically go on as soon as they experience a power drop below 45 volts. They will stay on for about fifty minutes and automatically shut off and begin recharging when power is restored. In addition, they become instantly available emergency flashlights when unplugged. Among the more definitive ways of dealing with a power failure is to have an auxiliary generator or wind-powered alternate electrical system.

Portable electric heaters are useful to have for brief fuel emergencies and to direct toward frozen pipes. A dry usable supply of sand mixed with salt and stored in a plastic garbage container is good for throwing on icy paths and stoops. (Do not overdo the salt near friendly shrubs and trees.) Telephone breakdown might lead to thoughts of a CB base station, ham radio, or Aldis lamp. However in these degenerate times, who has taken the trouble to learn Morse code? A battery-powered radio is also a good idea.

*LIGHTNING*   David's brother's house was hit, and part of the demolition was a vaporized downstairs telephone. Well-wishing people have often gently suggested that we not talk on the phone during electrical storms. That lightning bolt was sufficient emphasis for David.

# Plans For Coping

If you live in a house that is subject to any form of natural or unnatural disaster, we think you should have a plan for protection and/or evacuation. A fictional Dorothy was slow to get into the cyclone cellar and ended up in Oz. The reality, however, would probably have been far less entertaining. Use these pages for prethinking your personal safety, and the safety of the household.

*PLANNING PREVENTS PANIC*   Be aware of potential sources of disaster. In our area a major flood a few years ago washed out bridges and left many families isolated. It is useful to know alternate access routes, including footpaths and woodland trails. These are best checked out in non-stressful times.

hurricane:_____ other: _____

blizzard:_____ plans for emergency housing:

flood: _____

forest fire:_____

volcanic eruption:_____

earthquake:_____

mud slides:_____

nuclear disfunction:_____

tornado:_____

# NEIGHBORS
# AND
# RESOURCES

# The Neighbors

As we both started to think about our respective neighborhoods, we found that we had very little intimate, or for that matter nonintimate, contact with many of our neighbors. Of course today we live in a far more mobile society than existed even fifty years ago. Now people are able to travel large distances to see their friends and are therefore no longer dependent on the immediate environment for their social or even their mechanical lives. But even in a geographically expanded world, it is still useful to know who your neighbors are. You need not have intimate social contact with them. But should you see a strange truck backed up to an adjacent house or an unaccompanied eighteen-month-old toddling across your front lawn, it is helpful to have a working catalog of the neighborhood's statistics. Knowing your neighbors is also a way of recognizing strangers.

Neighbors vary. Some are friendly and useless. Some appear quite brusque, but are very handy in emergencies. This does not preclude the existence of friendly and useful and/or brusque and useless categories. Another sorting system is the "yes" and "certainly" people, the spontaneous refusers, the "I'd love to . . . butters," and the "if you'd only asked me at some other timers."

Once one of Sylvia's neighbors phoned at four in the morning to report that Sylvia's dog was in the process of turning over his garbage cans. She sleepily apologized and then, while on her way to take remedial action, tripped over her dog, who had been asleep all night in the hall. It would seem that the complaining neighbor didn't have an up-to-date neighborhood-dog-recognition chart and hence uttered an inaccurate accusation.

### NEIGHBORHOOD WATCH AND MUTUAL AID

1. In winter we always look to see that there is a reassuring plume of smoke coming from an older neighbor's chimney.
2. _____
3. _____
4. _____
5. _____

# And the Neighborhood

Whether you live in a house or a mobile home, perhaps you would like to make a schematic drawing or a map of your neighborhood, listing names, telephone numbers, and whatever other data you may consider useful. If you live in an apartment complex, your notations of your nearby community would be buildings and apartment numbers attached to the phone numbers of whatever dwellers you have contacted, along with those people responsible for maintenance. Again your neighborhood may be scattered or it may not even exist, but a map of your vicinity can help you relate to the inhabitants. We don't necessarily advocate gregariousness, but should an emergency arise, it is good to know names and telephone numbers.

You may decide to color friendly houses green, unfriendly houses red, and neutrals yellow, or whatever colors you happen to associate with various attitudes and emotions. You also might use some form of letter code, such as, *CPF* Close personal friends or *OBS* Occasionally borrows sugar.

# Who's Who

| name of neighbor | address | phone # | business phone # |
| --- | --- | --- | --- |
| | | | |
| | | | |
| | | | |
| | | | |
| | | | |
| | | | |
| | | | |
| | | | |
| | | | |
| | | | |
| | | | |
| | | | |
| | | | |

# in Our Neighborhood

| names of other members of the family | notes |
| --- | --- |
| | |
| | |
| | |
| | |
| | |
| | |
| | |
| | |
| | |
| | |
| | |
| | |
| | |
| | |
| | |

# People and Tool Resources

When a friend of ours left the service, he carried home a hand-operated tank-retrieval winch. It is heavy, cumbersome, and not something one uses everyday. However, when the contractor who landscaped around David's house got his bulldozer stuck in a swamp, this particular winch was a low-cost, energy-efficient solution to the problem. Knowing the whereabouts of a tool such as this gives one a sense of security.

There are certain tools that you do not lend to people, sometimes out of consideration for the tool, sometimes out of consideration for the people. Extension ladders are an example of a borrowable tool. Other shareables are canning equipment, building jacks, rigging equipment, block and tackles, dollies, come-alongs, long extension cords, and sump pumps. This list is not exhaustive. Chain saws, however, are three times more personal than toothbrushes and never lent.

In considering both the safety of the user and the safety of the tool, the lender has a responsibility to make certain that the borrower is aware of any and all risks involved. Sylvia once borrowed a small electric chain saw from someone who did not bother to do this. She was saved from almost certain decapitation by a dear friend, who happened by and would not leave until he had instructed her fully as to the saw's safe operation.

Certain friends are most easily kept by not lending them tools, and it is best to lend things only to people who are capable of, and willing to, replace them if they become either lost or damaged.

Older tools may turn up their toes at any second, and you have to take the attitude that this form of departure is not the borrower's fault. Sometimes it is best to accompany the tool as its operator. Other specific tools are totally irreplaceable and are best not let out of the owner's hands. David once borrowed a fine aluminum hand truck so as to move a refrigerator. It had two tired welds, which gave way even though it was being gently used. He did not bore the owner with this fact, but merely dropped it off at a heli-arc welder's for definitive repair. Check the condition of things before you borrow them, and if the item is about to head for tool heaven, it's probably better to borrow someone else's. Be a picky borrower, and as a lender and a borrower keep a record here of sources and dispositions. It is always good to decide how long a tool is to be away and also if it is returnable on demand. Going and getting it back yourself is a trip you probably shouldn't have to make.

| who | tool or capability | limitations | appropriate recompense |
|-----|--------------------|-------------|------------------------|
|     |                    |             |                        |
|     |                    |             |                        |
|     |                    |             |                        |
|     |                    |             |                        |
|     |                    |             |                        |
|     |                    |             |                        |
|     |                    |             |                        |

A friend is the person you phone at three o'clock in the morning to tell that your car is stuck in a snowbank. He answers, "Where?" not "How?" or "Why?"

One friend owns a fine metal detector, and he is a generous lender. He feels that a two-dollar contribution to the battery fund, or a six-pack is the considerate way to reward the machine.

# Tools Belonging To Our House

There are certain tools in our house that do not get loaned.

These tools do not belong to the bicycles or to the cars. They are the house's own and must never be removed for any reason. Ideally they have their own storage space and can even be color-coded with the house's own distinctive paint.

*AN INVENTORY OF TOOLS*   Add them up and shudder. They are worth taking care of, because the replacement value today is unbelievably high, and, even more important, some of the old favorites are no longer available. Many years ago David's brother hung all the family tools on a garage wall and then drew an outline of each, which he carefully painted red. It was a good idea. However, remodelings occur, and the wall's gone now, covered over with paneling. Only one of those original tools gallantly survives.

*FURTHER PRESENTS FOR THE HOUSE*   Knowing what tools you don't have is very important. A list of these can eventually be turned into useful tools you do have. Currently David needs a $5/16''$ socket for a $1/4''$ ratchet wrench. However, he does own three $19/32$- to $21/32$-inch open-end wrenches that don't seem to fit anything except the reverse pedal band adjustment nut on a Model T Ford.

*SEASONAL TOOLS*   These often tend to get slung away after use, and then as the year turns and their useful happy hour comes back, they are nowhere to be seen. Snow shovels and icebreakers aren't needed in the summer, but it is nice to know where they are when summer ends. This group includes pruning shears, leaf collection equipment, cider presses, sprinkling cans, and garden hoses.

*COMPOSITE TOOLS*   Some people think that hacksaws don't work, but that's because they've never tried one with a new blade in it. The chucks of most electric drills require a specific key to tighten them, and appreciate a good selection of bits that are sharp. Staplers need staples and mat knives need blades.

*TOOL ORGANIZERS*   A word of caution here. Before obtaining any of the commercially available systems, such as tool caddies, dial-a-drills, or even simple compartmented cloth rolls, see how well they work for others and be sure they relate to your own sense of order and the sort of person you are. Some of these arrangers often seem to further the cause of disorganization. Perhaps the best organizers are made by oneself for one's own specific tools.

| name of tool | size | brand name | serial # | model # | when bought | replacement cost |
|---|---|---|---|---|---|---|
| | | | | | | |
| | | | | | | |
| | | | | | | |
| | | | | | | |
| | | | | | | |
| | | | | | | |
| | | | | | | |
| | | | | | | |
| | | | | | | |
| | | | | | | |
| | | | | | | |
| | | | | | | |
| | | | | | | |

# Tools Borrowed

| what tool | owner | date borrowed | for how long | date ret'd |
|-----------|-------|---------------|--------------|------------|
|           |       |               |              |            |
|           |       |               |              |            |
|           |       |               |              |            |
|           |       |               |              |            |
|           |       |               |              |            |
|           |       |               |              |            |
|           |       |               |              |            |
|           |       |               |              |            |
|           |       |               |              |            |
|           |       |               |              |            |
|           |       |               |              |            |
|           |       |               |              |            |

WHITNEY'S HAND DRILL

# Tools Lent

| borrower | what tool | when lent | for how long | when returned | replacement cost |
|----------|-----------|-----------|--------------|---------------|------------------|
|          |           |           |              |               |                  |
|          |           |           |              |               |                  |
|          |           |           |              |               |                  |
|          |           |           |              |               |                  |
|          |           |           |              |               |                  |
|          |           |           |              |               |                  |
|          |           |           |              |               |                  |
|          |           |           |              |               |                  |
|          |           |           |              |               |                  |
|          |           |           |              |               |                  |
|          |           |           |              |               |                  |
|          |           |           |              |               |                  |
|          |           |           |              |               |                  |
|          |           |           |              |               |                  |

# Gardening

| tool | cost |
| --- | --- |
|  |  |
|  |  |
|  |  |
|  |  |
|  |  |
|  |  |
|  |  |
|  |  |
|  |  |
|  |  |
|  |  |
|  |  |
|  |  |
|  |  |

# Other Outdoor Tools

| tool | cost |
|------|------|
|  |  |
|  |  |
|  |  |
|  |  |
|  |  |
|  |  |
|  |  |
|  |  |
|  |  |
|  |  |
|  |  |
|  |  |
|  |  |
|  |  |

# Who Has One?

who has available certain things
which may only need to be used briefly
i.e. crutches, wheelchairs, baby furniture etc...

| who | what |
| --- | --- |
| | |
| | |
| | |
| | |
| | |
| | |
| | |
| | |
| | |
| | |

# FINDING THINGS

# Getting It Together

Living spaces differ. This is not the book of our tent, but rather the book of our house. Arabs move when camel droppings get too deep. This practice is called nomadism. Living on a twenty-six-foot sloop is different from living in the czar's old Winter Palace in St. Petersburg, where, after a bomb scare in 1907, a search determined that a peasant and his cow had been ensconced undisturbed in one of the rooms on the second floor for several years.

The rationale for mess is "If I leave it right here, I'll have it when I need it." With a lot of things piled around, it may look to you as if you're doing a lot. The reality probably is that you've surrounded yourself with a graveyard for misplaced and abandoned projects. There are people who never have time to file their papers or arrange their tools, but their endless searches consume infinitely more time than a systematic ordering would take. Hurry is often the handmaiden of disaster. In one set of false priorities, what needs doing immediately always takes precedence over preparation for future accomplishment. A further function of mess is what the Transactional Analysis people call Wooden Leg: "If only I didn't have this mess, I could really get started." Mess is one of inertia's staunchest friends.

We have all had the experience of spotting something that has managed to get into an unusual place and, as we pass, commenting about it to ourselves without replacing it. The inevitable outcome is a total inability to find the item the next time it is needed.

David has saved his entire correspondence, which stretches from childhood through his army service. He hasn't looked at these letters in thirty-five years, but if he ever wished to reconstruct those times, they would be invaluable. Should he ever decide to dispose of these letters, he would contact the people who sent them and ask if they had any interests in rereading them.

A collection of photographs of various members of the community appeared at the town dump. They had been taken many years ago. David found and retained them. He plans, some winter's evening, to sort through them and then write to the various identifiable people to ask if they would like to have this material.

There are different kinds of storage: immediately retrievable, sometimes needed, archival material, and the stuff you're never going to need for anything. This last category can be either sold, given away, or thrown away. Possessions eat space. However much room you have, if you keep filling it with things, you will run out. And don't clutter up prime storage space with little-used stuff.

Try to underload storage facilities. The dragon of chaos is a prolific breeder and must always be kept in check. Watch out particularly for rooms that are not being occupied, either by a person or by a function, especially if no assigned family member is responsible for their care. They easily become jammed with junk. A friend moved into this area, stayed five years, and then moved away, taking with him the same truckload of unlabeled anonymous boxes he'd brought with him and never opened, thereby discovering that over a five-year period whatever was in the boxes were things he obviously didn't need. Or were they just things he never used but felt a need to own?

Sylvia has developed a system of labeled cartons. She labels them on all sides so that they can be identified no matter what way they are stacked. They are labeled, Sweaters, Out-of Style Shoes, Off-season Shoes, Pants Too Tight, Summer Tops. The cartons are emptied and refilled as the seasons change. When her daughter, Heather, left for college in Oregon, she went one step further. She numbered her boxes and made triplicate lists of the contents of each. One was taped to the box, one went with her, and one remained with her mother. This way, if she wanted her mother to send her something, it could be accomplished with a minimum of difficulty.

Christmas decorations are a very interesting phenomenon. They are used predictably, regularly, and rarely. Make sure, before putting them away, that the lights are functioning and that you have extra bulbs, hangers, and whatever other nonreusable decorations you may want for next year. Especially since there are sales at the close of each holiday season.

Important occasionially used items should not be so hidden and hard to reach that your use of them is inhibited. These include dark-room supplies, children's toy trains, fishing equipment, and camping and picnic gear. Consider service pieces for large gatherings, such as punch bowls and hog-roasting machines. And how about your cider press?

A rusting cast-iron stove once camped in front of and slightly to one side of David's front door. It stayed there nearly nine months. It had been replaced and should have gone either to the dump or to a secondhand store the day it came out. It didn't, so it served to make his place reminiscent of those colorful backwoods establishments whose landscaping consists of gutted Volks-wagens, broken-down refrigerators, derelict washing machines, and burned-out dryers—the debris of civilization as we currently know it. In fact we tend to suspect that one abandoned object seeks and draws another ruined piece of equipment to its side, if only for company.

Storage can be thought of in terms of retrieval time: one second, thirty seconds, one minute, several hours. First-aid and firefighting equipment are "now." "Almost now" are items of daily living: cooking supplies, clothing, common tools, and replaceable hardware.

Certain storage areas do not work. They are either unapproachable or unarrangeable. David's low-ceilinged attic has an entrance that is always cluttered, and the windowseats with cushions covering them are clumsy and disorderly. If you are lucky enough to have a proper attic, keep a cleared space near the entrance as a staging area. Sort things there and then route them to their appropriate locations. Think about giving each family member his or her own clearly delineated space.

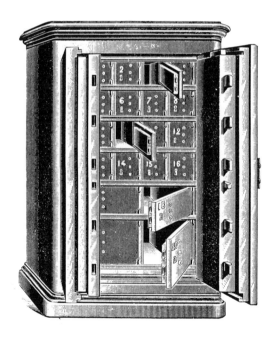

# Diagrams of Our Storage Space

# Things We Might Misplace

| item | location | item | location |
| --- | --- | --- | --- |
|  |  |  |  |
|  |  |  |  |
|  |  |  |  |
|  |  |  |  |
|  |  |  |  |
|  |  |  |  |
|  |  |  |  |
|  |  |  |  |
|  |  |  |  |
|  |  |  |  |
|  |  |  |  |
|  |  |  |  |
|  |  |  |  |

| item | location | item | location |
|------|----------|------|----------|
|      |          |      |          |
|      |          |      |          |
|      |          |      |          |
|      |          |      |          |
|      |          |      |          |
|      |          |      |          |
|      |          |      |          |
|      |          |      |          |
|      |          |      |          |
|      |          |      |          |
|      |          |      |          |
|      |          |      |          |
|      |          |      |          |
|      |          |      |          |
|      |          |      |          |
|      |          |      |          |
|      |          |      |          |

# ONGOING RECORDS

## RECORDS

### KEEPING TRACK
### OF IT ALL

# Insurance Policies

| type of policy | company | policy # | name of agent | agent's phone # |
|---|---|---|---|---|
|  |  |  |  |  |
|  |  |  |  |  |
|  |  |  |  |  |
|  |  |  |  |  |
|  |  |  |  |  |
|  |  |  |  |  |
|  |  |  |  |  |
|  |  |  |  |  |
|  |  |  |  |  |
|  |  |  |  |  |
|  |  |  |  |  |
|  |  |  |  |  |
|  |  |  |  |  |

# We Hold

| notes on coverage | location of policy | amount of premium | renewal date(s) | other |
|---|---|---|---|---|
| | | | | |
| | | | | |
| | | | | |
| | | | | |
| | | | | |
| | | | | |
| | | | | |
| | | | | |
| | | | | |
| | | | | |
| | | | | |
| | | | | |
| | | | | |
| | | | | |
| | | | | |

# The Furniture

| piece | date acquired | source |
|---|---|---|
| | | |

# in Our House

| cost | description and history | appraisals |
|------|------------------------|------------|
|      |                        |            |
|      |                        |            |
|      |                        |            |
|      |                        |            |
|      |                        |            |
|      |                        |            |
|      |                        |            |
|      |                        |            |
|      |                        |            |
|      |                        |            |
|      |                        |            |
|      |                        |            |

# Works of Art

| item | media | when acquired | source |
|------|-------|---------------|--------|
|      |       |               |        |
|      |       |               |        |
|      |       |               |        |
|      |       |               |        |
|      |       |               |        |
|      |       |               |        |
|      |       |               |        |
|      |       |               |        |
|      |       |               |        |
|      |       |               |        |
|      |       |               |        |
|      |       |               |        |
|      |       |               |        |
|      |       |               |        |

# in Our House

| cost | description and history | appraisals |
|------|------------------------|------------|
|      |                        |            |
|      |                        |            |
|      |                        |            |
|      |                        |            |
|      |                        |            |
|      |                        |            |
|      |                        |            |
|      |                        |            |
|      |                        |            |
|      |                        |            |
|      |                        |            |
|      |                        |            |
|      |                        |            |

# The Cherished Artifacts

| piece | when acquired | source | cost |
|-------|---------------|--------|------|
|       |               |        |      |
|       |               |        |      |
|       |               |        |      |
|       |               |        |      |
|       |               |        |      |
|       |               |        |      |
|       |               |        |      |
|       |               |        |      |
|       |               |        |      |
|       |               |        |      |
|       |               |        |      |
|       |               |        |      |
|       |               |        |      |

# in Our House

description and history          appraisals

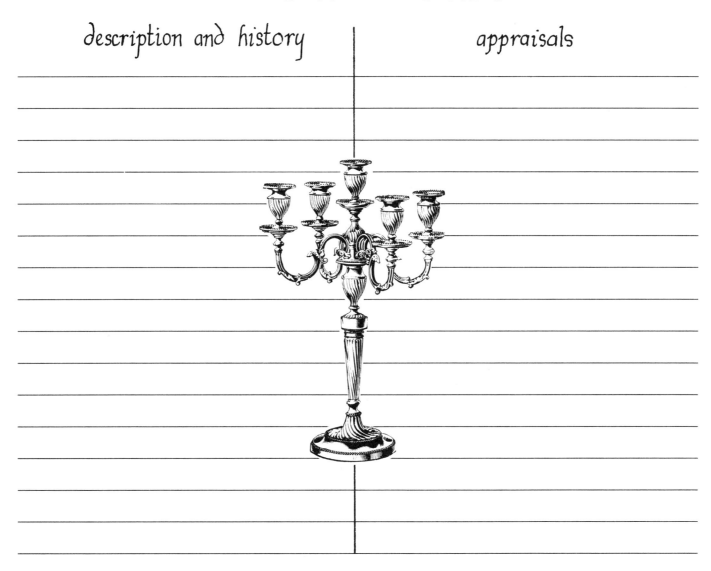

# Books That Belong

This is not the library of our house, but rather a special group of books, pamphlets, and maps specifically relevant to the enjoyment and the functioning of it. Certain regional books can enhance the appreciation of the area you live in. Some refer to the neighborhood's past history. Certainly there are specific volumes identifying local animals and plants, and possibly there is a pertinent geological guide.

David has the fifth edition revised for 1897 of *Rand McNally's Handy Guide to the Hudson River and the Catskill Mountains,* wherein the author mourns the loss of the old self-sufficiency he had previously noted in his account from the Centennial Year, ". . . replaced by worldly notions, ambitions and materials, introduced by the summer boarder and the fast mail."

David is not a sentimentalist but sometimes other people's feelings and thoughts help him to orient himself. All we are saying is, library sales and old book stores reveal rare books that may provide local information, a precious treasure.

In addition there are relevant geodetic survey maps and, if you live near the ocean, appropriate nautical charts and tide tables that can help you to experience your surroundings. A road atlas as well as a world atlas is useful. Various evocative catalogs and how-to books are filled with information. And are there favorite novels that your house might decide to cherish?

# With Our House

| title | author | publisher and date |
| --- | --- | --- |
| | | |
| | | |
| | | |
| | | |
| | | |
| | | |
| | | |
| | | |
| | | |
| | | |
| | | |
| | | |

# Disasters—

We hope that this page will remain blank for the next hundred years, but it's a good idea to know if there *have* been disasters. Sylvia's basement was always dry from the time she purchased her house in 1971. In 1979 a friend stored all her belongings down there, and that April a major flood ruined many of them. Had Sylvia known that there was a potential for flooding, she would never have thought of her basement as a facility.

# Natural and Man Made

| date | event | consequences | remedial action |
|------|-------|--------------|-----------------|
|      |       |              |                 |
|      |       |              |                 |
|      |       |              |                 |
|      |       |              |                 |
|      |       |              |                 |
|      |       |              |                 |
|      |       |              |                 |
|      |       |              |                 |
|      |       |              |                 |
|      |       |              |                 |
|      |       |              |                 |
|      |       |              |                 |
|      |       |              |                 |
|      |       |              |                 |

# Record of Fuel Usage

| date | quantity | unit cost | total | date | quantity | unit cost | total |
|------|----------|-----------|-------|------|----------|-----------|-------|
|      |          |           |       |      |          |           |       |
|      |          |           |       |      |          |           |       |
|      |          |           |       |      |          |           |       |
|      |          |           |       |      |          |           |       |
|      |          |           |       |      |          |           |       |
|      |          |           |       |      |          |           |       |
|      |          |           |       |      |          |           |       |
|      |          |           |       |      |          |           |       |
|      |          |           |       |      |          |           |       |
|      |          |           |       |      |          |           |       |
|      |          |           |       |      |          |           |       |
|      |          |           |       |      |          |           |       |
|      |          |           |       |      |          |           |       |
|      |          |           |       |      |          |           |       |
|      |          |           |       |      |          |           |       |
|      |          |           |       |      |          |           |       |

# In Our House

| date | quantity | unit cost | total | date | quantity | unit cost | total |
|------|----------|-----------|-------|------|----------|-----------|-------|
|      |          |           |       |      |          |           |       |
|      |          |           |       |      |          |           |       |
|      |          |           |       |      |          |           |       |
|      |          |           |       |      |          |           |       |
|      |          |           |       |      |          |           |       |
|      |          |           |       |      |          |           |       |
|      |          |           |       |      |          |           |       |
|      |          |           |       |      |          |           |       |
|      |          |           |       |      |          |           |       |
|      |          |           |       |      |          |           |       |
|      |          |           |       |      |          |           |       |
|      |          |           |       |      |          |           |       |
|      |          |           |       |      |          |           |       |

# Property Taxes

| year | assesed value | tax per thousand | school tax | county tax | other |
|------|---------------|------------------|------------|------------|-------|
|      |               |                  |            |            |       |
|      |               |                  |            |            |       |
|      |               |                  |            |            |       |
|      |               |                  |            |            |       |
|      |               |                  |            |            |       |
|      |               |                  |            |            |       |
|      |               |                  |            |            |       |
|      |               |                  |            |            |       |
|      |               |                  |            |            |       |
|      |               |                  |            |            |       |
|      |               |                  |            |            |       |
|      |               |                  |            |            |       |
|      |               |                  |            |            |       |
|      |               |                  |            |            |       |

# GROWING THINGS

# The Plants

| what plant | when and how to water |
|---|---|
| | |

# of This House

| best light | feeding required | other details |
|---|---|---|
| | | |
| | | |
| | | |
| | | |
| | | |
| | | |
| | | |
| | | |
| | | |
| | | |
| | | |
| | | |
| | | |

# Shrubs, Hedges and

| what planting | where obtained/date | cost |
|---|---|---|
|  |  |  |
|  |  |  |
|  |  |  |
|  |  |  |
|  |  |  |
|  |  |  |
|  |  |  |
|  |  |  |
|  |  |  |
|  |  |  |
|  |  |  |
|  |  |  |
|  |  |  |
|  |  |  |

# Clinging Vines

| location | requirements for happiness |
|---|---|
| | |

# The Trees Around Us

| what tree(s) | where purchased/date | cost |
|---|---|---|
| | | |
| | | |
| | | |
| | | |
| | | |
| | | |
| | | |
| | | |
| | | |
| | | |
| | | |
| | | |
| | | |

# Our Local Source of Oxygen

| location | requirements for happiness |
|---|---|
|  |  |
|  |  |
|  |  |
|  |  |
|  |  |
|  |  |
|  |  |
|  |  |
|  |  |
|  |  |
|  |  |
|  |  |
|  |  |
|  |  |
|  |  |

# Successful Plantings

| flower | from seed or flat | company name catalogue # | where planted? | date of planting | date of first flower |
|--------|-------------------|--------------------------|----------------|------------------|----------------------|
|  |  |  |  |  |  |
|  |  |  |  |  |  |
|  |  |  |  |  |  |
|  |  |  |  |  |  |
|  |  |  |  |  |  |
|  |  |  |  |  |  |
|  |  |  |  |  |  |
|  |  |  |  |  |  |
|  |  |  |  |  |  |
|  |  |  |  |  |  |
|  |  |  |  |  |  |
|  |  |  |  |  |  |
|  |  |  |  |  |  |
|  |  |  |  |  |  |

# of Annual Flowers

special nurturing techniques

notes for combining with other flowers
notes for future care; protection

# Vegetables and Fruits That

# Have Prospered in Our Garden

# Identification Map of

# Plantings on Our Property

# Our Lawn

| date | action taken | effectiveness |
|------|-------------|---------------|
|      |             |               |
|      |             |               |
|      |             |               |
|      |             |               |
|      |             |               |
|      |             |               |
|      |             |               |
|      |             |               |
|      |             |               |
|      |             |               |
|      |             |               |
|      |             |               |
|      |             |               |
|      |             |               |
|      |             |               |
|      |             |               |
|      |             |               |

# Its Care and Maintenance

| date | action taken | effectiveness |
|------|--------------|---------------|
|      |              |               |

# Enemies of Growing Things

-blights and insects common to our area, types of vegetation they affect, and insecticides etc. useful against them

# Chemicals We Have Used
# In Our Garden

| date | chemical | dosage | where used | purpose | effectiveness |
|------|----------|--------|------------|---------|---------------|
|      |          |        |            |         |               |
|      |          |        |            |         |               |
|      |          |        |            |         |               |
|      |          |        |            |         |               |
|      |          |        |            |         |               |
|      |          |        |            |         |               |
|      |          |        |            |         |               |
|      |          |        |            |         |               |
|      |          |        |            |         |               |
|      |          |        |            |         |               |
|      |          |        |            |         |               |
|      |          |        |            |         |               |
|      |          |        |            |         |               |
|      |          |        |            |         |               |

# Marvin's Garden

Our friend Marvin makes a yearly map of his garden. It shows what's planted, what varieties he planted, when he harvested, and some notes about insects and other pests, and failures. He also notes succession plantings. Marvin plants his smaller plants on the south side of his garden plot and the taller plants on the north side so the taller plants do not obstruct the sun from the shorter plants.

N↑ **taller plants this end**

corn
corn
corn
corn
corn — *pumpkins inter-planted*
corn

*horse radish (perennial)*

*asparagus (perennial)*

*cucumbers to climb here* ← *fence*

beets (Detroit Dark Red)
↕18″ radishes (Red Globe) 4/27 — followed by Bush Limas 5/30
↕18″ lettuce (oak leaf) 5/7 | New Zealand Spinach 4/21

*border of dwarf marigolds*

# Notes For Future Plantings

diagrams of borders and beds
we've seen and liked

and things that have worked
in our garden

# THE
# WORLD
# AROUND
# US

# Public Transportation

travel agent: _____

_____

railroad: _____

airport limousines: _____

airlines: _____  ferries: _____

buses: _____  other: _____

taxis: _____

# To and From Our House

current schedules

be aware that they
are periodically
changed

# Keeping Track of the Hours

The fantastic local air show at the Old Rhinebeck Aerodrome occurs weekends from June through September from one to six in the afternoon. The adjacent aircraft museum is open daily. The nearby Catskill Game Farm is open daily from April 15 through Labor Day, from nine to six. For local places that you are familiar with, you might wish to note their least crowded day. Keep the hours and dates of periodic local events and happenings.

There are also many services and facilities, such as aerobic dance classes, bicycle clubs, churches, synagogues, movie theaters, dentists, lumberyards, gas stations, maybe a take-out pizza parlor, and a bar that will cash your checks. You may not use all of these, but you never know when you will have guests who desire them.

On a Monday David's brother drove fifteen miles to the shoemaker's. Guess what day the shoemaker is closed?

# The Availability of Local Services and Facilities

| | Sunday | Monday | Tuesday | Wednesday | Thursday | Friday | Saturday |
|---|---|---|---|---|---|---|---|
| | | | | | | | |
| | | | | | | | |
| | | | | | | | |
| | | | | | | | |
| | | | | | | | |
| | | | | | | | |
| | | | | | | | |
| | | | | | | | |
| | | | | | | | |
| | | | | | | | |
| | | | | | | | |
| | | | | | | | |
| | | | | | | | |
| | | | | | | | |

| | Sunday | Monday | Tuesday | Wednesday | Thursday | Friday | Saturday |
|---|---|---|---|---|---|---|---|
| | | | | | | | |
| | | | | | | | |
| | | | | | | | |
| | | | | | | | |
| | | | | | | | |
| | | | | | | | |
| | | | | | | | |
| | | | | | | | |
| | | | | | | | |
| | | | | | | | |
| | | | | | | | |
| | | | | | | | |
| | | | | | | | |
| | | | | | | | |

| | Sunday | Monday | Tuesday | Wednesday | Thursday | Friday | Saturday |
|---|---|---|---|---|---|---|---|
| | | | | | | | |
| | | | | | | | |
| | | | | | | | |
| | | | | | | | |
| | | | | | | | |
| | | | | | | | |
| | | | | | | | |
| | | | | | | | |
| | | | | | | | |
| | | | | | | | |
| | | | | | | | |
| | | | | | | | |
| | | | | | | | |
| | | | | | | | |

# Good Shopping

a place to buy fresh seafood: _____

good fresh fruits and vegetables: _____

bakeries: _____

good deli: _____

favorite supermarkets: _____

butcher: _____

other food specialty stores: _____

_____

_____

interesting clothing: _____

_____

_____

_____

good clothing outlet stores: _____

thrift shops: _____

_____

# To Be Remembered and Shared

photography supplies: _____

 art supplies: _____

 craft materials: _____

 other hobby supplies: _____

 pet shops: _____

 tropical fish: _____

sporting equipment: _____

fishing equipment: _____ live bait shop: _____

gunsmith: _____

_____

other: _____

_____

_____

_____

# Eating

| name | location | phone # | type food |
| --- | --- | --- | --- |
| | | | |
| | | | |
| | | | |
| | | | |
| | | | |
| | | | |
| | | | |
| | | | |
| | | | |
| | | | |
| | | | |
| | | | |
| | | | |
| | | | |

# Out

| hours | recommended dishes | price range | ambiance |
|-------|--------------------|-------------|----------|
|       |                    |             |          |
|       |                    |             |          |
|       |                    |             |          |
|       |                    |             |          |
|       |                    |             |          |
|       |                    |             |          |
|       |                    |             |          |
|       |                    |             |          |
|       |                    |             |          |
|       |                    |             |          |
|       |                    |             |          |
|       |                    |             |          |
|       |                    |             |          |
|       |                    |             |          |
|       |                    |             |          |

# Local

golf: _____

_____

swimming: _____

_____

ice skating: _____

skiing: _____

_____

horseback riding: _____

_____

roller skating: _____

_____

bowling: _____

_____

tennis: _____

_____

boxing: _____

_____

# Sports

racket ball: _____

_____

pool: _____

_____

basketball: _____

_____

baseball: _____

_____

soccer: _____

_____

hockey: _____

_____

boating: _____

_____

fencing: _____

_____

horse racing: _____

# Bicycle Trails, Picnic Grounds,

| name of place | location | phone # |
| --- | --- | --- |
| | | |
| | | |
| | | |
| | | |
| | | |
| | | |
| | | |
| | | |
| | | |
| | | |
| | | |
| | | |

# Hiking Trails and Camping Spots

| facilities available | when open | fees | safe place to park | other |
|---|---|---|---|---|
| | | | | |
| | | | | |
| | | | | |
| | | | | |
| | | | | |
| | | | | |
| | | | | |
| | | | | |
| | | | | |
| | | | | |

# Places of Beauty or Special

| name | description |
|------|-------------|
|      |             |
|      |             |
|      |             |
|      |             |
|      |             |
|      |             |
|      |             |
|      |             |
|      |             |
|      |             |
|      |             |
|      |             |
|      |             |

# Interest in Our Area

| hours/times of year | admission | phone number | address / location |
| --- | --- | --- | --- |
| | | | |
| | | | |
| | | | |
| | | | |
| | | | |
| | | | |
| | | | |
| | | | |
| | | | |
| | | | |
| | | | |
| | | | |
| | | | |

# Wild Flowers, Trees and Plants

| plant | location | date discovered | date of bloom |
|---|---|---|---|
| | | | |
| | | | |
| | | | |
| | | | |
| | | | |
| | | | |
| | | | |
| | | | |
| | | | |
| | | | |
| | | | |
| | | | |
| | | | |
| | | | |
| | | | |
| | | | |
| | | | |
| | | | |

# Observed In Our Area

| plant | location | date discovered | date of bloom |
|-------|----------|-----------------|---------------|
|       |          |                 |               |
|       |          |                 |               |
|       |          |                 |               |
|       |          |                 |               |
|       |          |                 |               |
|       |          |                 |               |
|       |          |                 |               |
|       |          |                 |               |
|       |          |                 |               |
|       |          |                 |               |
|       |          |                 |               |
|       |          |                 |               |
|       |          |                 |               |

# Birds and Animals

# That Share Our World

# Other Nearby

# Creatures

# Hazardous Plants,

# Animals and Insects

# HOW TO  FIND US

# Where We Are

Amap of your own property, whether it be a city lot or many country acres, is a vivid way of seeing where you are. You may already have a survey map or plat to help you get started. In addition there may be an existing subdivision map that includes your property, or a larger-scale county map may be available. Usually all of these are impersonal and difficult to understand. We suggest that you translate them into a working map of your own design.

Boundaries are established by a surveyor, who generally indicates his or her qualified opinion of where you are by driving pieces of pipe into the ground. These markers are called monuments. In many older surveys monuments are vague. They can be a pile of rocks or a tree that was distinctive at the time but that by now may have been cut down or even have died on its own account.

As a child, David was walking one day in the woods and found a wagon axle stuck in the ground. Triumphantly carrying this treasure back to his father, he was promptly informed that he had just pulled up one of the corner monuments of the estate.

So it is useful to know the boundaries of one's property, particularly if you are building roads, fences, pools, or drainfields; planting gardens; or even cutting trees. Also consider this: If your neighbor's child should build a treehouse on your property and then fall out of it, breaking his neck, his parents might well sue you. The mere fact that you didn't know where your property was will not help you out in court.

# The Map We Have Made of Our Property

# Taking a Closer Look

If you have many acres, you may wish to make a detailed map of the immediate vicinity of your house, as a supplement to your larger-scale map. On it you can lay in the location of underground wiring, various pipes, and your wellhead. Describing such things in words and written dimensions is fine, but a map often gives a clearer picture. Include drainfields, plantings, electric meter, fuel filler pipe, and buried treasures if any. Keep it small and a treasure can be inexpensively installed. Or how about your own time capsule? Making maps enables one to take a very close look at where one is. Perhaps you know your latitude————and longitude————.

Walk with your small child over the grounds adjacent to your property, pointing out the features and landmarks that show the way home. Then draw up a map together. This most simple act of orientation may someday save the child from being lost.

Maps are not the easiest things to make. The first time around, your seven-year-old's may be better than yours. However, neither of these maps is the one that you will ultimately draw. It should be accurate enough to be usably descriptive, however there is always room for whimsy. A delightful map can be the basis of a Christmas card or a vignette on a family's stationery.

Sometimes it is nice to be able to locate an event that occurred in the past. Years ago David's brother once heroically killed a huge rattlesnake that was about to bite one of the neighbors. There is a photo showing the snake held out at arm's length. The dried rattles stayed around the house for a long time afterward. The snake was recycled as compost around the base of a large peach tree. The tree's gone now—a trace of the stump is all that remains—but the map is marked where that snake lies buried so as to make more vivid for grandchildren what would otherwise be just another old photograph whose meaning has been lost with the passage of time.

A magnificent old chestnut tree stood in death for many years. It is fallen now, but one of its branches still leans against a living tree and, unrotted, that chestnut wood has retained its strength and virtue for over sixty years. A possible cure for the disease that killed it was recently reported in the press. Along a nearby wall there remains a struggling clump of weedlike trees. They are the stunted descendants of another chestnut tree, crippled but not killed by the blight. This clump is on our map, so that we or someone else will be able to treat it whenever the cure becomes available.

# Directions to Our House

Even if you've lived wherever you now live for years, drawing a cogent map for getting to your house isn't easy. Try it, just from memory, on a piece of scrap paper. It helps to start with an already existing map. A trip to some local tourist-guidance center will often turn up specialized maps and brochures. Often there are national-park maps that may be adjacent to your home. If your house is somewhat older, it may be on a geodetic survey map, and if it is near the sea, is there a coastal and geodetic chart of your area?

Many joyous reunions and happy visits have been at least partially blemished by the various frustrations encountered when people become lost. We have found that the best guidance is given through a combination of graphic and verbal description, and we exercised a great deal of care so that words and pictures match. We have road-tested our directions, verifying distances with the car odometer and noting the actual wording and location of various signs. People approaching from different points may require specifically appropriate maps, and even with the best of directions, most still need encouragement and reassurance. So, it is sensible to locate nearby pay phones on the map. Give landmarks, both ones that indicate progress toward the destination and ones that indicate that a person has gone too far.

If ten outsiders have made the same error, be advised that your message is somehow defective or obscure. Once an apparently foolproof map is achieved, we suggest making copies. A map sent ahead of time can be the most sincere form of invitation, and a clearly shown destination is a good beginning for a happy journey. It can also save dollars in long-distance phone calls and uselessly burned gasoline. Visitors will be armed with a sense of confidence and will appreciate your thoughtfulness.

And of course some places are easier to get to than others. If somebody asks the way to Key West, one only need say, "Ride U.S. 1 south until it ends." People differ in their ability to give and take directions. Personalize the ones you give. Some people are auditory, some are visual, some need a bit of both. Ask your friends what works best for them. Recently a visitor called David from a nearby phone and, after listening to the directions carefully, suggested that insofar as David knew where he was being called from, the most simple homing device would be for the caller to follow David's truck home once it got to the phone he was calling from.

*AN INFORMAL TEST*  Name several places that are one, three, five, or any number of miles from your house. Next time you go to them, try your estimates against your car's odometer.

_____

_____

_____

_____

_____

_____

_____

_____

_____

_____

# OUR
# HOUSE'S
# PAST

# The History of Our House

Recently there was an account of the finding of a soldier's skeleton inside some deep hidden place in a house on Long Island. The shreds of uniform, the type of flintlock musket nearby, and two shattered ribs indicated that he had been wounded and had then crawled into this place to hide from the battle fought nearby nearly two hundred years before.

David's friend Gordie Morris was an avid collector of antique cars. He once discovered one, a 1910 Thomas Flyer, underneath a house. It had originally been a very early handmade mobile home. Various extensions and additions through the years had created layers that concealed it, the way a pearl enfolds a grain of sand. With endless jacks and beams and careful excavations, Gordie was able to extricate the car without harming its surroundings.

Not all houses have such dramatic histories or antecedents, but it is fun to look back and discover how a structure found its way through to the present. And of course if a house is new, then its inhabitants will write its history with their daily lives.

# Photos of Our House

# The People Who Have Lived
# In Our House

# The Pets That Have Shared
# Our House

# Reminiscences

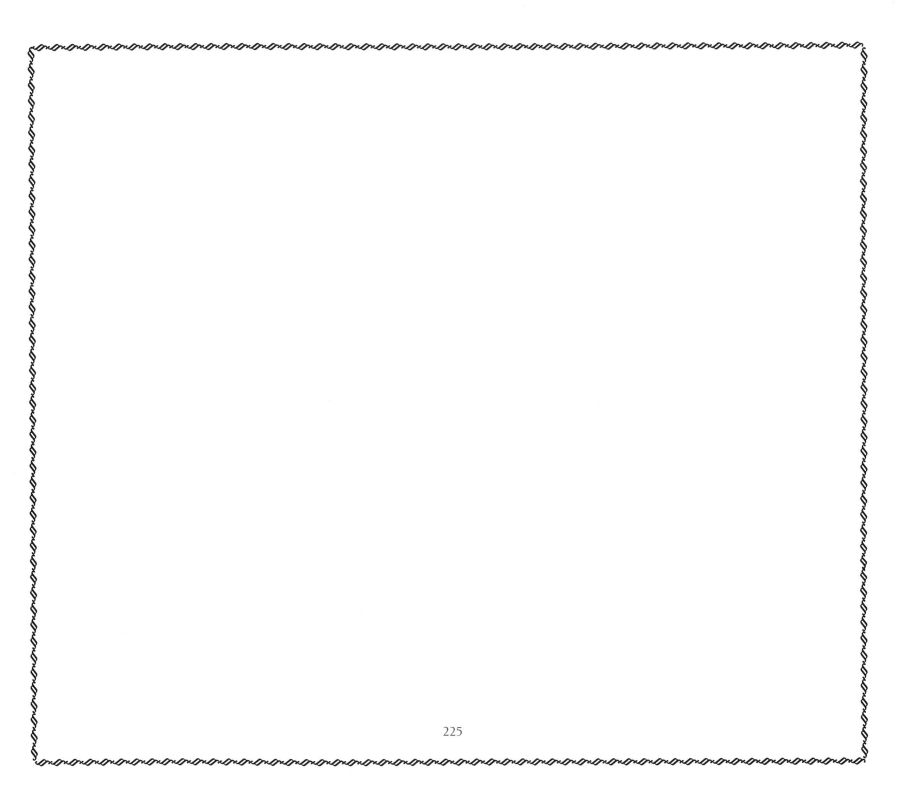

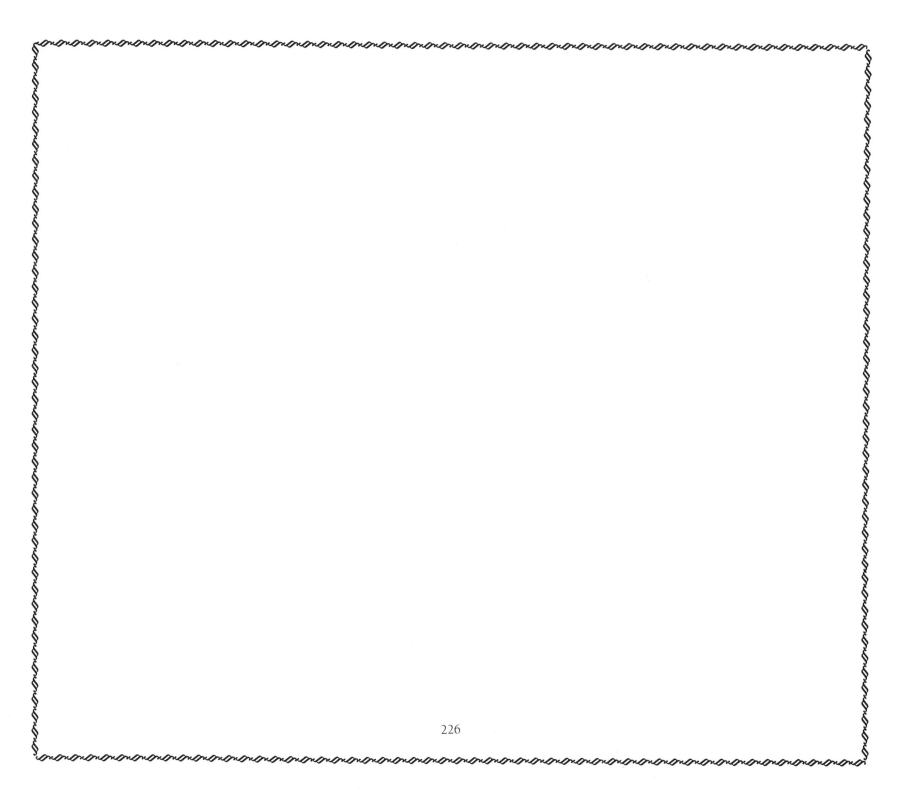

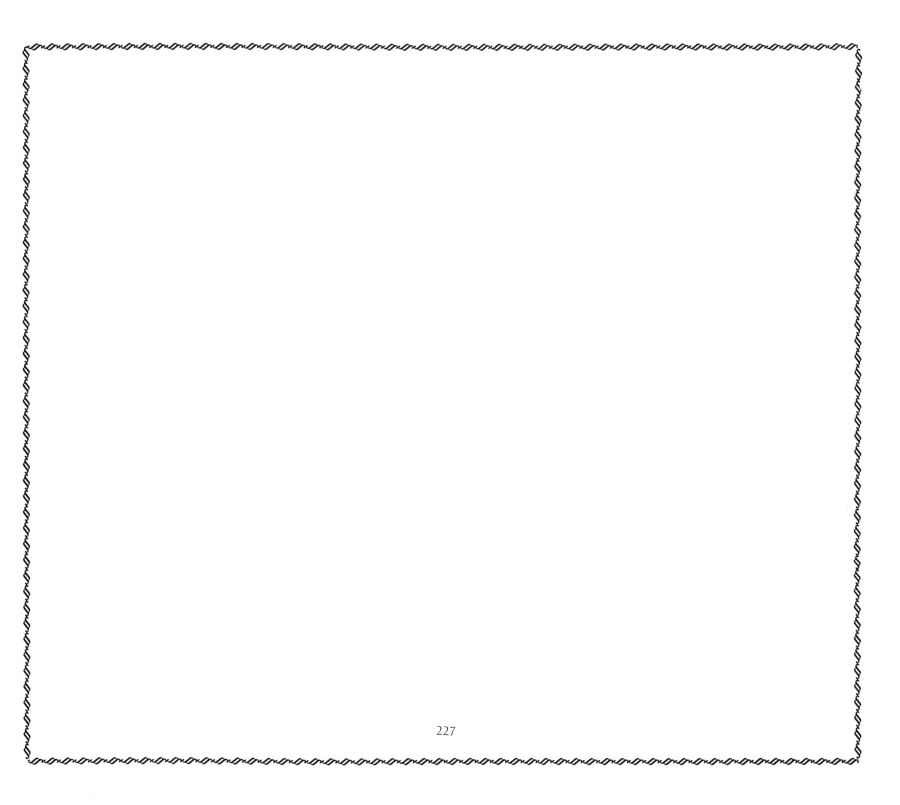

# Things We Still Need To Know About Our House

In older houses there may be many unsolved mysteries. Friends of ours recently purchased a colonial farm. They do not know if there is a basement beneath the kitchen floor. Several layers of linoleum may well have hidden a trapdoor entrance. For that matter, even newer buildings do not always reveal themselves completely. When Sylvia's washing machine empties, there is a strange gurgling noise from a pipe that sticks out of the dirt floor in the garage. It would be instructive to know where it goes to, because there is a dry well somewhere out there, and should it clog, it will have to be found. In the meantime she is reluctant to pour a concrete floor.

A friend just learned where the water meter was in her house after fifteen years of wondering why people left cards on her doorstep asking her to read it.

# Notes

# Notes

# Notes

# Notes

# Notes

# Notes

# Notes

# Notes

# Notes